Be

a

channel

Be a channel for our
Lord and Savior!

Paul A. Ferrel

by

John 3:16
" 14:6
I John 1:9

Paul A. Ferrel

To order my book call me at:
(563) 823-0567

Huntington House Publishers

Huntington House Publishers
P.O. Box 53788
Lafayette, Louisiana 70505

PRINTED IN THE UNITED STATES OF AMERICA.

Library of Congress Card Catalog Number
2002105321
ISBN 1-56384-198-3

All Bible references are from
The Living Bible unless otherwise identified.
Tyndale House Publishers
Weaton, IL. 1971

Contents

In Appreciation

"Thank you God for my lymphatic cancer and for Trudi Werner who inspired me to write this book myself; for without both, this book, as written, would not have come to fruition."

I owe much gratitude to those who assisted me with editing my manuscript in the earlier and later stages: Pauline Meyer, Lisa Ewart, and Kevin Holdsworth (final draft).

I greatly appreciate those who gave me leads on angel/spiritual stories: Delbert and Mary Ann Crawford, Lynn and Judy Lauritsen, Trent and Sharon Moore, Karla Thibeault, Dena Lyon, and Barbara Twomey.

I owe a debt of gratitude to those who shared their delightful angel/spiritual experiences with me, and they are recognized in the angel chapter.

I appreciate the numerous readers who gave me feedback as I labored to bring interest, inspiration, and a flow of continuity to my writing.

I dedicate this book to all of those who are staring death in the face, those who are scared, those who feel great uncertainty, those who feel overwhelmed with loneliness, and those who have lost all hope. I pray as you read the words in this book, written for you, that God's great, unconditional love, peace, comfort, and joy will permeate your being to its depth.

I also dedicate this book to my sons and daughter and to their precious families:

Mark & Diane Ferrel and grandsons Grant & Colin,

Roger & Donna (Ferrel) Hafner and granddaughters Marie & Michelle, and

Scott   D. Ferrel.

I

When the Bottom Fell Out of My Bucket

"And we know that all that happens to us is working for our good if we love God and are fitting into his plans."
—Romans 8:28

The warm morning sun was starting to peek over the low mountain range as I began my run through the Red Desert in early June of 1992. The cool, morning air was invigorating as I followed a path cut through the desert by various vehicles. It was usually a challenge to make it to my descent point without having to walk, especially when facing the usual, strong headwind that was nearly always present by mid-morning in Wyoming.

Later, as I returned home, I noticed some discomfort in my lower abdomen; however, it soon dissipated. My mind was on flying to Fairbanks, Alaska, in a few days where I was enrolled to take the necessary classes for recertification as a school psychologist in the state of Alaska. I had been employed as a school psychologist from 1988-90 with the Lower Kuskokwim School District in Bethel, Alaska. The district consisted of schools in Bethel, plus over twenty Eskimo villages, most of which were reached by small plane. With tundra all around and accessible only by plane or barge/boat in the summer, the area was known as the bush. It was my desire to return to Alaska, to fill my need for more adventure, better pay, and to satisfy my curiosity about that expansive, exciting land.

The next morning I was running my usual path, reflecting on the joy of having completed another school year and contemplating an enjoyable summer filled with running, hiking, traveling, and visiting my children. When I returned from my run, I again noticed some persistent discomfort in my lower abdomen. I also began running a temperature, having night sweats, and in general, feeling terrible.

Since I did not have a family doctor, I randomly picked a general practitioner from the phone book, which proved to be a very unwise decision, as I later learned that this doctor had once been sued for a wrong diagnosis. After suffering three days with these symptoms I saw him for a medical evaluation. My white blood cell count was at 33,000, with 3,000 to 10,000 being the normal range. He gave me a prescription for an antibiotic and sent me home. The antibiotics seemed to help a little, but I continued to have a temperature, night sweats, and a general uncomfortable feeling. Later, I was evaluated by an internal medicine physician. My white blood cell count was now down to 16,000; apparently the antibiotics I was still taking had caused this decrease. This doctor encouraged me to continue the antibiotics. Nine days and two physicians later, I called my oldest son, Mark, in Kansas at 5:30 A.M. to inform him that I was driving to the emergency room of the local hospital. A CT scan showed that my appendix had ruptured. Dr. Michael Werner, an excellent local surgeon, for whom I am very thankful, indicated that it appeared to have metastasized. He then operated that evening. Unfortunately, this was not the end of my medical problems as more tests and

Grant
(grandson)

symptoms were to follow. While still in the hospital, and on one of my most difficult days, Mark called to inform me that a school district in Alaska called and wanted to talk to me about a school psychologist position with them for the '92-'93 school year. I felt terrible and working was not on my mind. I never returned the call. My white blood cell count was still at 16,000 when the hospital released me. Instead of having a summer filled with running, hiking, traveling, and visiting with my children, it was filled with more doctors and medical procedures.

In July I was sent to the University of Utah Medical Center in Salt Lake City where they removed a lymph node from under my arm. In August they performed a bone marrow biopsy and a CT scan. Shortly before the '92-'93 school year began, when I would be returning to work as a school psychologist, I went to the medical center to hear the results. The diagnosis: non-Hodgkin's low-grade lymphoma cancer—stage four (very advanced). My reaction was, *how could I be in this situation? Me, a long distance runner for many years! I ate my green vegetables (steamed and raw), fresh fruits, little meat, kept fat intake to a minimum, and generally believed I ate pretty healthily. I didn't smoke or drink alcoholic beverages, except for an occasional glass of wine.*

My oncologist gave me three choices. I could do nothing. I could take chemotherapy pills, which would keep the symptoms down for awhile, but would eventually lose their effectiveness and would make it harder for intravenous chemotherapy to be as effective if we wanted to use this method later. Thirdly, I could go through aggressive chemotherapy. I didn't like any of the choices, but I desperately wanted to overcome the cancer so I chose the latter. I began a long period of uncertainty.

Days before the start of the school year, I stopped by

the special education department in the district office. For the first time, with wet eyes and a halting voice, I shared my health status with the secretaries upon whom I often relied to make my job run smoother during the course of the school year. The more I heard myself describing my cancer and what I was going through, the easier it was for me to accept the difficult situation I was in. I've always perceived myself as a lucky person, and I still felt this way; however, this was new territory for me.

In early September, I began my first of many, long drives (approximately 350 miles round trip) to Salt Lake City for my chemotherapy sessions. I had chemotherapy every Friday for three weeks, one week off, then the same regimen was repeated until I had completed eighteen sessions. I remember some of the medicines as nitrogen mustard, which badly scarred a major vein in each of my arms; methotrexate, which made me feel as though I was having the flu for about three days, and VP-16. I asked to have my therapy sessions on Fridays so I would have the weekend to recover. My first few sessions did not seem too bad, but as sessions progressed, I felt more averse to having to go through them. During the initial chemotherapy sessions, as the chemo dripped into my vein, I visualized the video game Packman going through my lymph node system and devouring every cell which had a "C" (cancer) on it. I tried to do this in a relaxed state, as I knew my mind was more receptive when I was relaxed. After a few sessions, though, I didn't feel like using my mental energy to do this, so I just closed my eyes and tried to relax as much as possible.

The bumps (enlarged lymph nodes) on the back of my neck and other places, as well as my enlarged spleen, decreased in size very quickly after one or two treatments. My oncologist seemed amazed at how well my body was responding. It gave me hope, but at stage four, with the cancer spreading throughout my lymph node system, cancer in my bone marrow, and cancer enlarging some of my organs, I thought it would be very difficult for the chemo to get it all. My oncologist and an oncological nurse both told me that I would lose my hair, which was already thinning considerably. I thought briefly about getting a hair piece but decided it was not for me.

I surprised them, losing some, but not a lot of my hair. Near the beginning of my chemotherapy I began taking what I hoped was a secret weapon that was going to help me overcome this disease. I believe this weapon was what kept most of my hair on my head. I'll share it later.

My mind continued to vacillate between preparing for death and getting things in order or just getting through all of the chemotherapy and hopefully, overcoming this cancer.

I continued to run a few times a week, three to five miles at a time. Running was one of my great joys in life, and I didn't want to lose it. Running mellowed me out, gave me a feeling of well being, and made problems in my life seem less important. Plus, I just liked to run and I liked the challenge of races, usually marathons (26.2 miles).

As the chemotherapy sessions progressed, I began noticing a shortness of breath and a pounding heart after walking up stairs at work. I was fortunate to be able to work throughout the school year without using many sick days, however, my running stopped in October, as I lacked the energy to continue. Because of my rolling veins, finding one to put an IV in became more and more difficult as the chemo continued. Generally, it took several attempts by the nurse(s) before they found a location in one of my veins which would work. I dreaded those @#!@ needles! It made for a very long and tiring day for me;

the long drive there, the blood tests, the waiting in the hospital, seeing my oncologist, the hour and a half chemo session, and then the long drive home, sometimes over treacherous ice and snow covered roads during the winter months.

Living alone, I found times when I felt it would have been nice to have had someone living near me who could assist me with making decisions when I didn't feel up to the task. I kept my focus on getting through the eighteenth and last chemotherapy session, which was 12 February 1993, a date that will forever be with me. It was a great relief to have gotten through it all.

On 19 March 1993 I went through more blood tests, another bone marrow biopsy, and another CT scan that would determine whether the cancer was gone. Again, my thoughts, at times, doubted that the chemo could get all of my stage four lymphoma cancer; it seemed too much to ask. My oncologist said he would call me at the beginning of the following week to let me know the results. He didn't, and feeling anxious, I called him the latter part of the week. He said, "It looks like we got it." It was a great relief! Most doctors say that if you make it through five years without the cancer reoccurring, you're pretty much home free. I hoped that with getting back to running and with what I thought was my secret weapon, I would never see the cancer again.

I praised God, was thankful for life, and was looking to the future with new hope. I made plans with my son, Mark, to go backpacking and camping in Colorado in early August 1993, something we tried to do each summer.

We hiked into the San Juan Mountain range north of Durango. On the trail we passed over the narrow gauge Durango & Silverton railroad line. We were surrounded by beautiful scenery, and the trail, at times, followed the clear and swift mountain stream. It was calming to see the water flowing rapidly and hear its sound as it rippled over the many rocks in the shallow stream. We cooled our tired, warm, bare feet in the cold, mountain stream. Mark enjoyed trying his hand at flyfishing, a new endeavor for him. We heard the steam whistle of the train and appreciated its beauty as we watched it pass slowly by. The passengers waved to us, and we returned their greeting. I immersed myself in the beauty of nature, the appreciation of life, and the thrill of being with my son as we shared this long-awaited camping trip.

When the fall of 1994 arrived I began a correspondence course through the University of Alaska in Fairbanks in an effort to prepare myself for my return to Alaska as a school psychologist. In May of 1995 I consulted with an ENT (ear, nose, and throat) doctor regarding the removal of my enlarged tonsils. He told me to come back in July when I returned from Alaska, and he would take them out.

In early June I flew to Fairbanks where I took a second course on campus. I interviewed with the Fairbanks School District while there. When I returned home, I saw the ENT doctor again. He noticed a change in my tonsils and chose not to remove them. He encouraged me to see my oncologist in Salt Lake City, whom I had been seeing every few months since overcoming my non-Hodgkin's lymphoma in early '93. When I returned home, after seeing the ENT doctor, my daughter-in-law called to tell me that I was to call the Director of Special Education with the Fairbanks School District. I gave a lot of thought to my situation before returning the phone call because I believed the director was going to offer me a school psychologist position for the upcoming school year. I had little doubt that my cancer had returned. When I called her she asked if I was still interested in a position with their school district. I told her about my health problem and that there was a real concern that my cancer had returned. I thanked her for the job offer, but told her that it would be better for me to remain with my present school district because of my health problems.

Two days later I saw my oncologist. He was sure that my cancer had returned. I was devastated! I made the long drive home in quiet. "Dear Heavenly Father, I'm getting tired of the struggle. My running regimen and secret weapon let me down. Lord, I still praise you for your beautiful world and for your great gift of eternal life! How fortunate we are!"

Life goes on, and I had to go on too. It was the only reasonable option I could see. Lacking sufficient money on which to retire, I had to keep working to support myself and prepare myself financially for retirement, assuming I would make it until then. Having grown up as a child in a home with barely sufficient financial assets, at least I could leave my three children a fair amount of money from my estate. If I didn't live much longer, at least I felt good about being able to help them financially, to make their lives a little easier.

My goal was to work for ten years with the school district so I could keep my health insurance, and retire in the year 2000 when I would turn sixty-one. As I write this book, my retirement is about two years away. I thought that it would be pneumonia that might do me in, and I've had pneumonia two of the last three Christmas seasons.

Since the cancer is in my immune system, I recognize that it will be harder for my body to fight off colds, infections, and pneumonia as the cancer advances. Since I work with many children in my job, I realize that I am vulnerable to catching their colds and infections. Elementary kids seem to always have plenty of colds during the course of the school year.

It was disheartening that the cancer had returned,

but all was not lost as things transpired which gave me hope. We all have to hang on to hope. *"Let us hold unswervingly to the hope we profess, for he who promised is faithful"* (Heb. 10:23, NIV, emphasis added).

The Cause of the Culprit

As I reflect on back before my cancer was diagnosed, I feel confident that I have a likely answer for why I got this type of cancer. There has been little cancer on either side of my family and no non-Hodgkin's lymphoma that I am aware of. So why do I have it? I believe I pushed myself too hard when I prepared for marathons, greatly fatiguing my body, which made me vulnerable to colds and infections.

I started running at the age of thirty-nine, running with Mark when he ran to keep his weight down for high school wrestling. It was at that time that I decided that life was passing me by, and I wanted to travel, do challenging activities, and experience new things. It was then that I set a goal for myself to run the Boston Marathon at the age of forty. I didn't make it to Boston when I was forty, but I did in 1982 at the age of forty-three, the same year Salizar won by two seconds over Dick Beardsley, the second-place finisher. It was a thrill to run up Heartbreak Hill and hear the speakers blasting a recording of Vangelis' "Chariots of Fire" and to have the great satisfaction of having run in the Boston Marathon!

With a running base upon which to train for a marathon, I usually started my training about four months before the race. I would slowly increase my weekly mileage until I was running 45-50 miles per week, which was usually the maximum for me and probably a minimum for adequate marathon preparation. I would try to do a little speed work on a track or interval training during shorter runs. I usually ran my long run very early on Saturday or Sunday morning. My long runs would range from about 12 miles early in my four-month training, then up to 22 miles the month or so before the marathon. I would run my long run almost every weekend, which was a mistake. I pushed myself too hard to make sure I could handle the marathon's 26.2 miles. I was aware that my body felt tired as race day drew near, but I felt if I slacked off on my running considerably the week before the marathon, I would be all right. When I let my body get so fatigued, I believe it greatly weakened my immune system.

In the mid 1980s, when I lived alone in Iowa City, Iowa, I was training for my fourth Twin Cities' (Minneapolis-St. Paul) marathon, which is held every year in October. Many large charter buses would take us to the starting line in Minneapolis before morning light. Many runners waited in the large lobby of the Pillsbury Building before the race started, keeping us out of the chilly morning air. When the race began, there was competition between the many water/aide stations along the route, as well as small groups of musicians that played for us as we traversed on the streets of the two cities. We also ran along paths, which on non-race days, carried bikers, joggers, walkers, and roller bladers. The route passed by lakes, which added to the enjoyment of the delightful, fall day, as we ran toward the finish line in St. Paul.

I would drive up to St. Paul on Saturday, the day before the race, and twice I was able to get tickets to see Garrison Keillor's "A Prairie Home Companion," which was broadcast over public radio for several years. The show was always the night before the marathon. Quality musicians, often off the beaten path, would be guests on the program. Garrison Keillor, an excellent story teller, would have a short segment on his live radio program where he would tell a descriptive and humorous mythical story about the Norwegian Lutherans in the community of Lake Wobegon, Minnesota, and the need for shy people to eat Powdermilk Biscuits, which . . . "Give shy persons the strength to get up and do what needs to be done." Mr. Keillor would always describe Lake Wobegon at the end of his story as the place . . . "Where all of the women are strong, all the men are good looking, and all the children are above average." "A Prairie Home Companion" is again back on the air after being off for a few years.

The fall is a beautiful time to run a marathon in the mid-west with the cool nights, warm sunny days, no more bugs, the crunch of colorful leaves under foot, and the sight of the beautiful fall foliage with leaves of vibrant shades of red, yellow, and orange. It is a time when you see and hear the Canada geese honking as they fly southward in their distinct "V" formation.

I developed a very bad cold two weeks before what was going to be my fourth Twin Cities' Marathon. I couldn't run for five days, and when I did go for a short run, I knew immediately that something was wrong. It was like the air was bouncing in my lungs. I had medical tests (X-rays, ultrasound, physical exam, etc.) done. My diaphragm was elevated on the right side, pushing up my right lung. The doctor concluded that a virus had damaged the nerves going down to my diaphragm/right lung area. He said it might be permanent or it might correct itself. Since then, X-rays have shown that my right lung is again correctly positioned. Needless to say, I did not run the marathon, and I had what seemed like a chronic cold until the following spring. I've had difficulty recovering from colds/viruses ever since. This all took place in 1985, about seven years or so before I was diagnosed with non-Hodgkin's low-grade lymphoma, which is a very slow-growing cancer.

I strongly believe that when I pushed my body in

training, particularly those very long runs, it greatly diminished the capability of my immune system, which includes the lymph nodes, to the point that when the virus hit, my body was unable to sufficiently fight it. I firmly believe this allowed the cancer to get a foot hold in my lymph nodes.

In June of 1998 Mark and I flew to Florida to be with my youngest son Scott. It was a joy for me to be with them as they scuba dived at Key Largo and West Palm Beach. Near the end of our stay in Florida I began not feeling well. Upon returning to Kansas with Mark, I immediately went to the emergency room at the Topeka Hospital. They diagnosed me as having bronchitis, and I began taking antibiotics. I continued to struggle with cold symptoms and coughing spells since this diagnosis, and it is now late November.

On 23 November 1998 I traveled to Salt Lake City to see my oncologist whom I hadn't seen since June 4th. Having to go for regular checkups is a constant reminder that my cancer is ever present. I was disappointed with the news, although it was not unexpected. My oncologist said my lymphoma cancer seems to be growing faster and that my kind of cancer is very hard to eliminate. He said if it was high-grade (fast growing) lymphoma it would be easier to eradicate. While there, he sent me back to the hospital lab to have several more vials of blood drawn from my arm and for chest X-rays. He set it up to have me come back in early December for my sixth CT scan. I later canceled this as I didn't feel up to driving 350 miles round trip, have the CT scan technician poke me a few times in her attempt to get the IV to work, which would allow the dye to disperse throughout my body prior and during the CT scan, and having to drink the milky chalky contrast during my drive there. I felt we had enough information already, so why the necessity of putting me through another long, tiring, stressful, and expensive day?

The day after Thanksgiving, 27 November 1998, I headed out early in the morning to Jackson, Wyoming, a three hour drive. I wanted to get away briefly, with plans of returning home the next day. I wanted to do some shopping, have some great meals, visit the elk refuge and habitat for swans, ducks, and Canada Geese, see the beauty of Jackson displayed during the Christmas season, enjoy the great beauty of the snow-covered mountains in the Jackson Hole area, and, particularly, to reflect on God and spiritual matters.

As I was driving around Jackson Friday evening, the starter went out on my car. On Saturday, I had it towed to a repair shop, and the shop owner/manager told me it would be Monday before they could start working on it. He indicated that it might be Monday, Tuesday, or even later before it was repaired. "Okay, God, you know I wanted to spend time with you, but let's not over do it," I thought to myself. However, as I lay in the motel room bed on Sunday morning, lots of thoughts for my book flooded my mind. It was very unusual for me to travel with my laptop computer and the disk containing my book, but on this occasion I had brought them along. I scampered out of bed and began writing down my many thoughts. I felt my thoughts and ideas were God-inspired, and I have since felt God has inspired me with words and ideas on other occasions as I write this book. Thus, good came out of my car trouble. I returned home late Tuesday afternoon.

On 14 December 1998 I went back to Salt Lake City to see my oncologist. While there, I started my first of five consecutive days of Fludarabine, another chemo. Two nurses poked me only four times, about average for me, before they got the IV to work for the chemo. The Fludarabine would be less damaging to my body; however, it was possible it would be less effective than the chemo I experienced in '92-'93. We just hoped to knock the cancer down for awhile.

The thought of just letting nature take its course was entering my mind with greater frequency. One day I may say, "Enough, no more!" to harsh chemo with its many negative side effects, to IVs which add to my stress, to long drives to Salt Lake City, to vials of blood being drawn frequently from my arms, to X-rays, to CT scans, to drinking the milky, chalky contrast prior to CT scans, to oncologists, to bone marrow biopsies, to medical procedures, and to the great expense to my insurance company and to myself.

Information on Fludarabine from the National Cancer Institute indicated that this drug will decrease my killer T-cells for up to two years. Killer T-cells help us fight off infection, viruses, pneumonia, etc. My immune system was already badly compromised so I wondered if I could afford to have my immune fighting capabilities diminished even further. I had serious pneumonia a year ago, and I continually struggle to fight off colds. I told God, "Lord, the outcome is in your hands. I put my trust fully in you. It's okay."

Chemo sessions two through five were given to me in Rock Springs at the local hospital. I greatly appreciate not having to make the long trip to Salt Lake City for all the treatments. On day five I received my last treatment and would repeat the whole process beginning 14 January 1999.

On therapy session number five, there was the nurse— goggles over her eyes, a mask over her mouth and nose, rubber gloves on her hands, and the whole front of her body covered with a type of apron. I felt naked in comparison! She was getting ready to put the harsh chemo in my body while she was protected to the hilt! She began her duties of trying to get an IV needle in a vein in my left arm as I lay there on a patient bed in one of the hospital rooms. She got the second IV poke to work, but in her haste to remove the rubber tourniquet from around my forearm, she caught the IV with her hand, damaging the IV. Thus, my stress level was elevated as another nurse assisted in getting me poked six times before success was found. One of these days as the painful point of that, seemingly huge IV needle penetrates my tender skin under my forearm, they may have to scrape me off the ceiling. However, since I'm of small stature, maybe they'll only need a pooper scooper! I felt sick when I left the hospital, and the ill (flu like, without the vomiting) feeling continued for four days.

After five days of Fludarabine I saw little decrease in my enlarged lymph nodes. I had expected my body to respond well to the chemo. Disappointment became a great possibility. After putting my body through all this unpleasantness it would be a severe challenge to my faith if Fludarabine provided little or no benefit.

On 14 January 1999 I saw my oncologist in Salt Lake City. He said he could detect a decrease in my enlarged spleen and liver, both enlarged because of the cancer. My white blood cell count was now at 7,000. My oncologist said it would take some time, but he saw signs that the Fludarabine was working. Also, he noted that I would have to receive Fludarabine each month for six months, going through five, consecutive days each time (thirty chemo sessions).

I had a bad cold (bronchitis) going into my five days of chemo in March. Even though I had just been put on an antibiotic, it became a real challenge for my badly compromised immune system to overcome the infection. I was in the local hospital emergency room twice and ended up being placed on my third antibiotic after not fully completing the regimen for the two previous ones.

After thirty straight days of being on an antibiotic, I was again placed back on antibiotics after being off of them for eight days. My bronchitis symptoms had persisted through a total of fifty-three days of antibiotics in March, April, and May. I missed nineteen days of work, and spring break saved me from using another six days of sick leave.

During one of these days when I was running a temperature, my bronchitis at its peak, and my body permeated with the harsh chemo, I called Leslie. She was the nurse who often came to my home to administer the Fludarabine to me, and she had encouraged me to call her anytime I needed help. She assisted me in trying to decide what we were going to do to get me through this. Leslie said, "Paul, you're beginning to worry me." She was always diligent, competent, and professional in her duties. It was a *God send* to have her come to my house where I could receive the chemo and her help in the comfort of my peaceful, cozy home. After she took my temperature, I said, "I feel terrible. I understand why people give up the struggle." Leslie asked softly, "Are you there yet?" With tears in my eyes, I responded weakly, "No." "Dear Lord, give me a courageous heart and keep my spirit strong."

For days uncertainty weighed on my mind. It seemed the outcome was teetering in the balance. On strong antibiotics, and filling my body with lots of liquids and plentiful vitamins, I provided my body with all the ammunition I could think of. Jesus was frequently in my thoughts and believing in His promise, I *knew* He was there to give me comfort and strength, whether or not I felt His presence. I wondered if I was ever going to overcome the cold symptoms, but then I recalled that God has a plan for me, and I did not believe it was God's plan for me to not make it through this.

The deeper the valleys we experience on our life's journey, the greater the opportunity for fully appreciating new heights. It provides us with a greater range of human emotions, gives us the opportunity for meaningful emotional, mental, and spiritual growth, and adds depth to our character. God, working through us, can use these attributes to nurture others when they struggle to make it through their valleys of life.

With the end of the school year approaching and summer weather ahead I looked forward to the long respite, and I hoped my body would fully recover from the trauma it had been through and increase in strength. The chemo and bronchitis combined had taken a lot out of me physically. Still, I was thankful that the chemo Fludarabine was available for use against my cancer.

All of us have experienced or will experience times during our journey through life when things happen which are out of our control, when the bottom falls out of our bucket. During these times we need to pray to God for guidance, do all we can ourselves, and turn the trial over fully to God, trusting Him to do that which is in accordance with His will. Knowing that God loves us with unimaginable, unconditional love, we can be assured that He'll do what is best for us.

II

My Secret Weapon

At the beginning of my chemotherapy treatments in 1992, a co-worker loaned me a book which she said Hospice uses. I liked the book so much that I went out and purchased a copy for myself. The book is, *Love, Medicine & Miracles*, by Bernie S. Siegel, M.D. He shares numerous stories regarding how one's attitude toward one's cancer or health situation can have a tremendous impact on overcoming or surviving it. He mentioned certain vitamins (antioxidants) which can help facilitate the body in overcoming cancer and other diseases.

Also, near the beginning of my chemotherapy treatment, a colleague loaned me the book, *Vitamins against Cancer*, which was replete with information on the vitamins and minerals our body needs to be healthy. It recommended much of the same vitamins mentioned in the *aforementioned* book, but in addition, it gave recommended dosages. I gleaned out of the book the vitamins I felt I needed to add to my diet to maximize my body's effort to fight off this cancer. I began taking these vitamins within the first month (September 1992) of starting chemotherapy, and I believe this was the reason that I lost little of my hair, which is a rarity for people who go through aggressive chemotherapy. The following was my daily regimen during chemotherapy:

Vitamin C— Usually 15,000 to 17,000 mg daily; buff-
             ered and time released over 12 hours. I usu-
             ally took 5,000 mg at breakfast, 3,000 mg
             at noon, 5,000 mg with the evening meal,
             and 3,000 mg at bedtime.
Vitamin E— 800 I.U.s daily (400 I.U.s twice daily).
Vitamin A— (Beta Carotene)—50,000 I.U.s daily
             (25,000 twice daily).
Selenium—   200 mcg (micrograms) daily (100 mcg
             twice daily).

Other items I also took:

1. COQ10 (Coenzyme Q10)—30 mg four times a day.
    COQ10 is supposed to help build up the immune
    system plus it provides numerous other benefits.
    Book—*The Miracle Nutrient Coenzyme Q10*

I purchased Coenzyme Q10 and many of my vitamins at the following address:

        Bioenergy Nutrients
        6565 Odell Place
        Boulder, CO 80301-3330
        (1-800-627-7775)

Bioenergy indicated that their Coenzyme Q10 comes
from Japan, reportedly, in its purest form.

2. During the last two months of my chemotherapy, I
    started taking garlic capsules, two twice daily. I un-
    derstand garlic contains germanium which is sup-
    pose to induce the production of interferon, which is
    sometimes used in cancer treatment.

3. Amway Double X multiple vitamins—I took one
    round tablet and one oblong tablet twice daily.

Herbs which are supposed to stimulate/enhance our
immune system:

1. Astragalus—One of the major herbs used in Chinese medicine, but under a different name in China.
2. Echinacea—An herb used by the American Indians (those on the plains). It should *not* be taken when you have a disease of the immune system, according to literature from the health food store.

I was taking about everything I could find which was supposed to enhance the immune system, including Echinacea, but I stopped taking it when I read that it is not recommended for people with a disease of the immune system. I wrote this regimen down after successfully overcoming my cancer the first time. Doctors have told me, arrogantly sometimes, that the vitamins were a waste of my money. This may or may not be true, but there is supporting evidence for much of what I have listed here. I believe doctors receive little training in nutrition in medical school so many may not be the most knowledgeable about vitamins.

I feel that in this country we should be spending considerable money on learning how to prevent some of these dreaded diseases. If we placed much greater emphasis on prevention of diseases it would be much more cost effective than trying to treat and/or cure them. However, hospitals and some of the medical professionals would not receive the huge financial benefits they now enjoy.

I perceive many people are more health conscious than years ago, but at the same time, we have a high percentage of people in America who are considerably overweight (nonmedical condition), have poor diets, and exercise little. I believe we have to take charge of our own health and do all we can to have healthy bodies.

What kind of care would we give to a Rolls Royce if we owned one? We would likely pamper it to the nth degree. We would keep it washed and polished, see that the interior is always immaculate, steam clean the en-

gine periodically, drive it only in fair weather, and keep it
garaged when we weren't driving it. Our body (including
our mind) is much more valuable than any Rolls and will
usually work well for us if we only give it the correct
treatment. How many of us are willing to put forth the
effort to make sure our body, our most prized possession,
is getting proper care so it functions well physically, mentally, emotionally, and spiritually?

It was a couple of years after going through aggressive chemotherapy and shortly after my oncologist told
me that my lymphoma cancer was back that I read the
book, *Spontaneous Healing,* by Dr. Andrew Weil (Harvard
educated). He expressed concern about taking antioxidant supplements during chemotherapy treatments. "If
you decide to proceed with radiation or chemotherapy,
discontinue use of antioxidant supplements during treatment, since they may protect cancer cells along with normal cells. Resume the supplements as soon as treatments
ends."

I don't know whether or not all of the antioxidant
vitamins (C, E, Beta-carotene, and Selenium) and other
supplements helped maintain some of my cancer cells or
not, but that's water over the dam at this point. This
information just left me feeling frustrated. It just comes
back to the idea that the patient, me in this case, has to
do all they can to figure out how to arm themselves with
sufficient knowledge so they can assist in overcoming their
own health problem(s). I feel we can't always count on
medical personnel to have all the answers or always make
the correct decisions for our health. We need to take an
active part in our own health care. Physicians and medical personnel are not equal in their knowledge and skills,
some are very competent and some should not be allowed to practice medicine on a dog.

A potential option for knocking down and/or putting my lymphoma into remission is the drug Bexar. It is

in stage III trials, and I have been following it for a couple of years. Bexar is specifically for low-grade non-Hodgkin's lymphoma patients who have had a relapse, which applies to me.

On NBC's "Dateline" 1 November 1998 they showed a segment on non-Hodgkin's low-grade lymphoma. Dr. Mark Kaminski, at the University of Michigan Cancer Center, has done a lot of research on the drug Bexar and its results on patients with non-Hodgkin's low-grade lymphoma. Dr. Kaminski reported that in their trials they are getting 71 percent remission rates. After seeing the "Dateline" segment, I called his office and talked with his oncological nurse. She indicated that Bexar should be on the market by the summer of 1999, after six months or so of study and approval by the FDA (Food & Drug Administration). Bexar is produced by Coulter Pharmaceuticals in California (1-800-823-7003).

Dr. Weil also expressed concern that people who have gone through chemotherapy may have damaged immune systems because of the harshness of the chemo. If this is the case, then even if somehow I'm able to totally overcome my lymphoma, I'll have to continue to deal with my weakened ability to fight off colds, pneumonia, etc.

Dr. Weil has a section in his book (Chapter 14) where he lists an eight week program for optimal healing power. In Chapter 19 (pg., 274) he also notes this:

Regardless of whether you choose conventional or alternative treatment, there are general recommendations that everyone with cancer should follow:

> • Because it represents failure of the healing system, cancer even in its early and localized stages, is a systemic disease. Patients must work to improve general health and resistance by making changes on all levels: physical, mental/emotional, and spiritual.

• As a minimum, I recommend changing diet according to the principles reviewed in. . . . Chapter 2; maintaining a program of regular exercise; taking antioxidant supplements; using tonic herbs, especially those with immune-enhancing effects; learning visualization or guided imagery techniques to help the healing system contain the cancer; working to heal relationships (with parents, children, and spouses, for example); and making whatever changes in lifestyle are necessary to give yourself the best chance for healing to occur.

• In addition, try to find people who have experienced healing of cancer, preferably those who have had your particular kind of cancer. Read accounts of healing and books that increase your confidence in your own healing capacity.

• Seek out healers. Get all the help you can find.

There seems to be a marked increase of new drugs on the market within the last few years and this year (1998) especially. President Clinton signed a bill which expedites new drugs being approved and getting them to those that need them, and this gives me hope as well as it should for you if you are in a serious health situation. Even though I can feel many enlarged lymph nodes throughout my body (pre-Fludarabine treatment), I trust that things will work out, even though I know not how. I am thankful that I'm able to continue working and that my type of cancer does not hurt, at least not at this point.

Things You Can Do to Enhance Your Overall Health
(Emotional, Mental, Physical, and Spiritual)

Read the Bible.

Pray.

Exercise regularly.

Get a massage.

Develop a support system.

Go for walks.

Enjoy your kids.

Spend quiet time alone.

Reduce/eliminate junk food, etc.

Get away for awhile.

Plan healthy fun things to do.

Have regular checkups—especially if you're older.

Know your body—check out anything unusual.

Get enough sleep/rest.

Keep life as simple as possible.

Manage your thinking so you don't upset yourself.

Do anonymous kind things for others.

Forgive yourself and others.

Know what is important in life.

Try to always do what is right.

Read spiritual material.

Meditate.

Eat healthy balanced meals (whole grains, fruits, etc.)

Use relaxation techniques.

Spend time in nature.

Enjoy your grandchildren.

Enjoy your pets.

Listen to relaxing music.

Use positive/spiritual affirmations daily.

Do something you enjoy.

Consider supplementing your diet with vitamins.

Make a list of ways to improve your well being.

Be flexible.

Don't waste energy on things of little value.

Be creative—make or do things with your hands—crafts, etc.

Daily give sincere compliments to those around you.

Live in the present, but plan ahead.

Find things for which to be thankful each day.

Enjoy your time with
friends and loved ones—
plan so it's successful.

Be generous.

Go to a zoo or museum.

Feed ducks in a park.

Keep your focus on Jesus.

Be patient—wait upon
the Lord.

Begin saving at an early
age.

Again, keep life simple.

Allow others to help you.

Help others in their time
of need.

Learn to play a musical
instrument.

Know that Jesus is *always*
with you.

Know that others will not
always behave as you
desire—allow them this
right.

Have a playful spirit.

Avoid those who are detrimental to your sense of
well-being, who drain
your energy.

Laugh as much as possible—
find humor in daily life—
laugh at yourself.

Walk on a beach.

Know you're loved uncon-
ditionally by Jesus.

Be humble.

Invest your money wisely
(growth funds and/or
growth equities).

Don't let material things
burden you down.

Have *reasonable* expecta-
tions for yourself and
others.

Let go of reliving mistakes
of the past.

Believe in and trust yourself.

Respect yourself and others.

Shy not from taking risks.

III

Lord, You're Talking to Me!

"An effectual fervent prayer
by a righteous man availeth much."

—James 5:16 (KJV)

I believe the spirit of God is within each one of us and is ever present to guide and comfort us if only we will listen. Jesus said, *"Lo, I am with you always, to the close of the age"* (Matt. 28:20, RSV). He gave us a comforter, the Holy Spirit, who lives within us. There have been times when I felt God's presence working in my life, guiding me in the direction He wanted and needed me to go. He was there to comfort me when I was struggling emotionally and had lost all hope.

Dag Hammorskjold was Secretary General of the United Nations when he was killed in a plane crash in Africa in 1961. That same year, posthumously, he was awarded the Nobel Prize for Peace. He wrote, *"The more faithfully you listen to the voice within, the better you will hear what is sounding outside."* I believe God, through the Holy Spirit, plants little seeds, gives us little signs, puts thoughts in our heads, and nudges us in the direction He wants us to go. I believe God sometimes works through others: friends, enemies, children, strangers, all types of people, and situations in an effort to communicate with us. But we have to listen, and we must be receptive to the signs. It is when we look back on our life that we can really see how things seem to have come together, how our path may have changed for the better, or we viewed things in a more productive way. But it is the choices we make which will help us find God, and He tries to guide us in ways which will help us find him. *"Ask, and you will receive; seek and you will find; knock, and the door will be opened to you"* (Matt. 7:7, TEV*). "In those days when you pray, I will listen. You will find me when you seek me, if you look for me in earnest"* (Jer. 29:12-13).

Francis Thompson was born in 1859 and died in 1907 more or less penniless and with few earthly possessions. He was the son of a physician and at some point in his life he became addicted to opium (form of heroin), which was sometimes dispensed to patients by his father. He wrote the original poem, *The Hound of Heaven,* which is still popular to this day. In 1997 Gordon McDonald did a contemporary translation of the poem. He wrote this about Francis Thompson:

> I have this irresistible feeling that the Francis Thompson, who strayed about on London streets, scrambled to make a penny or two in order to survive, and surrendered once and again to the seduction of drugs would have been unwelcomed in most churches, in most respectable communities, and in most of our lives. Yet, one cannot read this remarkable piece of poetry and not be impressed with the fact that beneath tattered clothes and untoward behavior lay a heart that was desperate to find order in life and peace with God. (pg., 79)

Francis Thompson writes in the poem about a God, even though he didn't mention Him directly, who re-

Marcene (sister) at Long Lake

lentlessly pursued him, and no matter how Francis tried to hide, negotiate, and run from God, God was never far behind. As a hound dog relentlessly pursues its prey on the trail, God relentlessly pursued Francis until He caught him. At the end of the poem, Gordon McDonald's translation, *The Hound of Heaven—A Contemporary Translation of a Timeless Masterpiece,* reads:

> Who is there who will love you in all your brokenness? Only Me; only Me. Please understand that those things which I have denied you were not taken that you might suffer harm, but rather that you would one day seek these things from Me. As might a child in a moment of loss think that everything is gone forever, you are tempted to think that life is over. But, it is not. Everything awaits you *at home.* Arise, take My hand; come home.

> Now the One who was always pursuing from behind is alongside. The chase is ended. I sense a darkness. Is it danger? No, it is rather the shadow of His hand of affection reaching out to me. And, this One who has chased so relentlessly after me says, 'You who were so foolish, so blind to the truth, so utterly weak: *I* am the One whom you have always sought in all of your furious *searches for security, well-being, and wholeness.* "You find all you want and need when you walk with Me." (pgs., 66-67)

On the Odyssey television channel on 31 January 1999, Dr. Gerald Mann, minister of the Riverbend Church in Austin, Texas, made reference to Francis Thompson's poem. Dr. Mann said, "God pursues us, not for his good, but for our good. God pursues us doggedly. God pursues us lovingly. God is a God who chases us patiently. And He waits and waits and waits until we come home. God just kept chasing me until He caught me."

Jesus talked about how He is the Good Shepherd and we are His sheep. If one is lost He will search until He finds the lost sheep (us), and He brings him/her home to safety. Jesus/God pursues us until we turn from our sinful lost ways and seek Him. He never gives up on us, no matter how much we mess up our lives, and He does His part in being available so we will come to believe and trust in Him, becoming dependent upon Him for all our needs. Jesus said,". . . *apart from me you can do nothing*" (John 15:5, NIV).

In life we want to make our own decisions and do our will, not God's will. We want to be in control, and we think we always know what is best for us. When we're young, we want to do what we want anytime with little regard sometimes for the consequences. Those males who think they are macho seem to believe they can solve a lot of their problems with muscular brawn. Those with wealth can often throw money at their problems and have them disappear. *"Tell those who are rich not to be proud and not to trust in their money, which will soon be gone, but their pride and trust should be in the living God who always richly gives us all we need for our enjoyment"* (1 Tim. 6:17). Some seem to believe they don't have to rely on God for assistance and guidance.

But there are times when we have little or no control over matters in our life, such as serious injury, terminal illness, loss of a job, loss of loved ones to death, etc. During these times we can expect to find ourselves in emotional, mental, and spiritual anguish, but these are also times when our emotions, soul, and spirit have a grand opportunity for growth, a time to allow ourselves to be caught by the pursuing God as we turn to Him. Little happenings in my life planted the seeds which brought me to God.

I grew up on a small and very modest farm in south-eastern Iowa. We had kerosene lamps until the summer after my eighth grade year in school. We never had running water, and we had coal/wood stoves. During those cold winter nights the fire in the living room stove would go out, and the next morning we would sometimes find a thin covering of ice in the water bucket in the kitchen. I can remember, even in high school, my father, older brother, and myself picking and shucking corn in the fields with a team of horses pulling the wagon during the cold winter months.

We never went to church; however, I can remember as a young boy going to Bible school a couple of summers at a Methodist church, which was located in the country among the many farmsteads. This was my first exposure to God and the Bible.

I can still remember painting a little plaster-of-paris dog sitting on a small square platform during one of our craft activities. I painted it white with black spots.

I attended a one-room country school (Des Moines Township #8) from kindergarten through eighth grade. I recall a time when a man in a suit came into our school and gave all of us little Bibles, something that would not be possible today. I remember how we could get little rewards for memorizing Bible verses. I can still recall memorizing the well-known verse, John 3:16 (KJV), *"For God so loved the world that he gave his only begotten Son and whosoever believeth in him shall not perish, but have everlasting life."* How precious this gift is!

After graduating from Fairfield High School in 1957, I went to boot camp at the Marine Corps Recruit Depot in San Diego. It was considered an all Iowa platoon (#363), though, as I recall, we had a couple of young men from Illinois. I attended church services at the recruit depot a few times, perhaps another seed from God to draw me to Him, even though I used some of the church service time writing letters home. The church was a peaceful and safe place, away from my drill instructors (DIs), where they didn't have the opportunity to yell at me. Since Sundays were usually a time for maintaining our gear and writing letters home as we remained in our quonset hut, that is how I spent most of my time.

It was 1963, when I lived in northeast Iowa and was married with three children. We rented one of two houses on a farmstead located among the many rolling hills a few miles north of the small town of Elkader, a scenic place with a very old, arched, stone bridge across the little river which flowed through the center of town. A couple rented the other house on the property, and the man once invited me and my family to attend their church services the following Sunday. He asked me if I knew where their church was located, and I told him I did, but I had the wrong church in mind.

The following Sunday we went to a congregational church for services, the church I thought he was talking about. I commented to my wife that I wondered where he and his wife were. It was later that I realized we had attended the wrong church, which happened to start services the very same time as his. I suspect God guided us into this church for a reason. We attended the congregational church on a regular basis, and we became friends with the minister and his wife. They had two junior high boys who were very knowledgeable about the Bible. The minister came to ask my wife and I if we would teach the Sunday school junior high class, which consisted of his two boys and one or two other children. My wife knew something about church and Bible stories as she had grown up attending a Methodist Church, at least some of the time. I felt quite ignorant about Bible stories, yet it didn't seem to bother me too much at the time. Since my wife knew some of this, and since we prepared the lesson prior to the class, I guess we did all right in presenting each lesson.

There was a particular Sunday school lesson about Gideon in the Old Testament. Gideon was instructed by God to take his army into battle (Judges 6:36-40). Gideon wasn't sure about God's message so he said to God, "If you are really going to use me to save Israel as you promised, prove it to me this way: I'll put some wool on the threshing floor tonight, and if, in the morning, the fleece is wet and the ground is dry, I will know you are going to help me." And sure enough, the next morning, this was the way it was. Gideon still had doubts about taking his army into battle, so he said to God, "Please don't be angry with me, but let me make one more test: this time let the fleece remain dry while the ground around it is wet." And the next morning, this was the way it was. It was after this lesson that I prayed for a sign from God that I could believe.

I remember one evening before going to bed, I prayed for some kind of sign that I could believe there is a God. I was very sincere, and I mentioned it to no one. I never even thought about telling my wife, as it just seemed natural for it to be just between God and myself. The next morning I got out of bed, not thinking about my prayer the night before, and walked into the living room. We had an outside storm door and then the front door, which entered into the living room. The inside door was open about a foot and as soon as my eyes focused on the opened door the thought was in my head, *"This is your answer."* One would have thought that this sign would have satisfied me, but the following night I again prayed for a sign that I might believe there is a God. The second morning I got up, again not thinking a thing about my prayer the night before, and as I walked into the kitchen, I saw water droplets on top of the stainless steel hood

over the stove. Again, the instant my eyes focused on the
water droplets, the thought was there instantaneously,
"*This is your answer.*" We lived in the house three years,
and I found it too coincidental to have prayed for a sign
two consecutive nights and to have experienced those
two occurrences the following mornings and with the
same thought; "*This is your answer.*" In three years I never
again saw those occurrences. I've never prayed for a sign
for God's presence again, and I have thought many times
about this special, spiritual experience. It has been reassuring and a source of strength for me. I praise God for
this experience, and it was a time in my life when I felt
very close to God.

I quit my job as a building inspector for Grinnell
Mutual Reinsurance Company, and our family moved
from the Elkader area to a small town near Cedar Rapids, Iowa. With borrowed money and veteran's benefits
from being in the Marine Corps, I enrolled in computer
programming classes at Kirkwood Community College
in Cedar Rapids. After about six months of school, they
hired me to operate their IBM 360 mainframe computer.

We soon moved to a rented house between Cedar
Rapids and Iowa City. I began taking college classes at
Kirkwood, and I continued to run the computer from 4
P.M. until midnight during the week. During my last quarter at Kirkwood, when I was working to complete my
two-year associate degree, my life became very stressful.
I would get up about 6:30 every morning. We only had
one car, so I would drive my wife to the university hospital in Iowa City where she was being trained as an oper-
ating room technician. Iowa City was about ten or twelve
miles from our home, and Cedar Rapids was about 15
miles in the opposite direction. After dropping my wife
off, I returned home where I got our two oldest children
ready for school and the bus. My youngest son and I
headed for Cedar Rapids where I dropped him off at a

day care, and I then went to Kirkwood where I was taking 11 quarter hours of classes. After class, I went to pick up my youngest son, and we went to Iowa City to pick up my wife. I returned them to our home, then I went back to Kirkwood to operate the computer until midnight. Monday through Friday I repeated this process.

It was a great relief when the quarter was over. I had been running on little sleep, and I could not seem to relax. I saw our family doctor, and he prescribed Valium for me. It mellowed me out, but I found myself not functioning very well emotionally. I had never felt this way before. I was losing affection for my wife and interest in previously enjoyed activities. I enrolled at the University of Iowa that fall and continued to struggle emotionally, with anxiety and some depression. I made it through two years at the university, which culminated in a Bachelor of Science degree in Psychology.

During the summer of 1973, I rented a small apartment in Emporia, Kansas in preparation of attending what is now Emporia State University in the fall. I was enrolled to take graduate classes in school psychology. I planned to come home on the weekends, a several hour drive to our home near Iowa City. The idea was not very practical as I look back on it. Before my first week of classes was up, I withdrew from the college. I knew I was not functioning very well emotionally. I just wanted to go home and get some kind of decent paying job which didn't require a lot of thinking. I guess I can be thankful that I had the energy and sense of responsibility to continue to make an income for my family.

Back home, I acquired a third-shift job at a meat packing plant, cleaning up blood and scraps of meat from conveyor belts, cutting saws, floors, etc. with large high pressure water hoses. Having little affection for my wife, it was fine with me to work third shift so I was not home nights, and I slept during the day when my wife was working and our kids were at school. I was withdrawn, didn't want to socialize, and continued to not function very well emotionally. In time my wife was able to talk me into seeing a psychiatrist. I saw him two or three times to talk, and the medication he put me on slowly began to help bring me out of the depression, but the damage was done in the marriage.

There was a time during my depression that I took a walk down the lane and through the pasture and into the timber area behind our country home. Finally, I sat down on a large, old, barkless tree trunk which laid on the ground beside a small, dried-up spring. I felt miserable emotionally. I prayed, thought about God, and dwelt in my emotional and mental anguish. After a while, I began my slow journey back home, and as I was walking on an incline in the pasture area, the following phrases came to me, one right after the other:

> *Jesus believes in me.*
> Trust him.
> Jesus loves me as I am.
> Jesus is within me.

Again, I've thought about these phrases many times over the years, especially when life became stressful. I believe these phrases were inspired by God.

In 1975 we moved to Emporia where I received my M. S. Degree in school Psychology, and my wife received a registered nursing degree. We moved back to the Iowa City area in 1978. My wife and I were divorced in early 1983.

God is still working in my life. It was in December of 1995 that my son Scott had a spiritual experience which involved me. He resigned his position as a crime scene investigator for the Sheriff's Department in Ogden, Utah. With his '91 Ford Ranger pulling a small U-Haul trailer and his gentle black lab dog with him in the cab, he headed out for a long tiring drive to Gainesville, Florida. He was going to be with his girlfriend who lived there, and he had hopes of securing a law enforcement position there. It was about 5 A.M. in the morning as he entered St. Louis. It was dark, raining, and for some reason, his truck was going through excess fuel, indicated by his dash board light. Scott said he began praying, and at some point, a spiritual message in the form of a voice instructed him to pass a message on to me and a friend of his back in Ogden. Scott said, "No." to the voice twice, but when the voice repeated the instructions a third time, he said he would do it. Part of the message was for Scott to share some information with a friend of his in Ogden. He was also instructed to tell me that he loved me, that God has a plan for me, and that I'm not to be so resistive. I was excited for Scott that he had this spiritual experience, as I know he'll think about it many times throughout his life, and it will be a source of strength and reassurance for him.

Later, I began wondering if God's plan for me was that my time on earth was drawing to an end. After a few weeks I asked Scott about this. He said, "No, I don't think so because it had positive feelings associated with it." Even though I believe death can be perceived as a positive spiritual experience if we are prepared, I sensed that this is not the plan God had in store for me at this time. I thank God for his plan for me, and I believe that God has a plan for each one of us. We just need to seek God and listen to that small inner voice which will guide us. When I feel discouraged with my health problems, I am lifted when I know that God loves me enough to have a plan for me. I know that God's plan for me is better than any plan I could devise, so I look to the future with hope. I'll know what the plan is if I make the effort to listen and watch for His guidance. "For I know the plans I have for you, says the Lord. They are plans

for good and not for evil, to give you a future and a hope"
(Jer. 29:11).

It was during my spring break in 1997 that I was in
Kansas visiting my son Mark and his family. I decided to
go to a Methodist church in Osage City, Kansas for Easter Sunday services. As I completed dressing in their
home, I put a twenty-dollar bill in my shirt pocket, which
I was going to put in the collection plate during services.
In the small county seat town of Osage City I parked a
short distance from the church. I checked my pocket to
make sure I still had the twenty-dollar bill. It was not
there! I happened to have another twenty in my pant's
pocket, so I put it in my shirt pocket. I went to the Easter services at the church, placing the money from my
shirt pocket into the collection plate. Following church
services I returned to my car on that beautiful, sunny,
Easter Sunday. As I sat behind the wheel preparing to
leave, I happened to see something on top of my small,
paper, garbage sack, which was nearly full of debris. It
was a twenty-dollar bill. I know I didn't throw away a
twenty-dollar bill! I felt God was saying to me, *"Paul, I
don't want your money as much as I want you."*

Prayer is an instrument by which we attempt to communicate with God. It is where we ask forgiveness for
our sins and wrong doings, where we share our concerns,
where we petition God to meet our needs, and where we
thank and praise Him for His greatness and for the positive things in our lives, no matter how small. And, yes,
we even need to praise and thank Him for our trials and
challenges as they provide us with a grand opportunity
for emotional, mental, and spiritual growth; bringing us
closer to our Lord and Savior. Everyday we can all find
things for which to be thankful to God. There can be
great power in the results of prayer as the Bible says, *"An
effectual fervent prayer by a righteous man [woman] availeth
much"* (James 5:16, KJV).

Many people have said they were praying for me as I was going through the many chemotherapy sessions in 1992-93 and also since the return of my cancer. I thank them and God for the many prayers which have been said on my behalf. I know there can be much power in prayer, and I know when we are staring death in the face, it takes a lot of faith and courage to pray for God's will to be done. In life threatening situations it becomes easy for us to pray for healing or survival if the thought of dying seems too scary and uncertain. The answer(s) we get from prayer is often not as we desire. We want things our way, but our will needs to become God's will.

"Mankind must suffer in darkness and blindness until of its own desire it surrenders self-will and becomes identified with the will of God. This will of God working out in individual and nation alike manifests as love, goodwill, brotherhood, justice, truth and peace." (pg., 69). *The Path of the Soul* by White Eagle.

In the tiny book, *The Quiet Mind,* sayings of White Eagle, he states this about the need to submit our will to God's will:

> Do not be discouraged. Learn not to be disappointed in anything, or any person. You are disappointed because your will, your desire, has been frustrated. Learn to submit to the Divine Will, for His Will is all-wise. Wait, then, for *His* appointment, learning to tread the path wisely, serenely.

> It is natural for the lower self to resent pain and suffering; but when you can surrender to God, so that your heart overflows with love and acceptance of the wisdom of God's plan, then you can make real progress, and you are filled with deep peace which is beyond the power of the world to give.

God never fails His children. Do not seek for things to work according to your desires; or for your circumstances to be arranged according to your earthly will. But have faith that God is leading you on the path to ultimate happiness.

Learn to bow to the will of God, remembering that there is an acceptable time of the Lord. God is infinitely wiser than His children, and His plan is perfect; His plan for your life is spiritual growth and spiritual unfoldment. When you are ready, that which is prepared will be placed before you. (pgs., 80-81).

Jesus came to earth to show us what God was like and to die on the cross for our sinful nature. He paid the price for all of our sins and wrong doings so we could be saved into eternal life. Jesus wiped our slate clean so God sees us as perfect if we trust and believe in Jesus and by God's grace. When Jesus was in the Garden of Gethsemane and His crucifixion was imminent, He prayed with such fervor that He sweated blood. He prayed to God that He would not have to do this (die on the cross), but He also prayed that it was to be God's will, not His (Luke 22:41-44). Praise God for this!

It was the latter part of May of 1948 that I had just completed the third grade at Des Moines Township #8 country school. I still have a strong, visual image of where I was at and an association of that image with a tragic event. I can still see the rather large, rectangle-shaped field located on my uncle's farm. There was my father on the tractor, planting at the far end of the field on a beautiful, sunny, spring day as I first stepped onto the tilled land. I was probably bringing him some water in a fruit jar with a lid, but I'm unsure about this. I no doubt overheard my parents and relatives talking about this tragic event, and for some reason, I associate it with the visual image of seeing my father working in that particular field.

The tragic event concerned a very small child, a girl I believe, who must have been about two or three years old. She had fallen down into the narrow shaft of an old abandoned well that was not capped. Many people seemed to be working feverishly to dig down to where she was in the shaft in order to rescue her. From the perception of my young mind it seemed that many people across America were praying for her safe recovery as people worked diligently throughout the night to save this little girl. She didn't make it.

No doubt many of us, during the course of our lives, have prayed for things to turn out certain ways and believed that it must surely be God's will too, but the results were not as such. It leaves us questioning why God did not help or intervene. There are other times when miracles seem to happen after prayers are given.

We just have to put our trust in God and go on faith. If we could see and understand both our earthly lot and Heaven simultaneously, we would be reassured and in awe. If we are spiritually saved because of trusting Jesus as our Lord and Savior, by faith we know that Heaven will be a place of great, unconditional love, joy, and peace; so much more than our small earthly minds can even fathom. "Thank you Lord!"

IV

Life Is Not Easy—
Praise God!

"Rejoice always, pray without ceasing,
give thanks in all circumstances; for this is the will of God
in Christ Jesus for you."

—1 Thessalonians 5:16-18, RSV

Life is not easy. It has its mountain tops and its valleys. We can all handle those mountain tops in our lives when everything is flowing smoothly for us, with special joys, triumphs, successes, attaining goals, and contentment. But it is the valleys of life that we need, even though we don't want to go through them, because they offer us a great opportunity - the opportunity to grow spiritually, mentally, and emotionally. Can we not be thankful to God for this opportunity before us? Within every valley there are seeds of opportunity for growth, and by growing, we in turn become a more effective vessel through which God can utilize our growth to touch others in a positive and spiritual way. Without this spiritual, mental, and emotional growth we are a less effective instrument or channel through which God can work. The more available we are for God's use, the more He can accomplish and the more love and joy we experience.

Over my many years of running, the lyrics of a Bob
Seger song would often come to mind, especially when
facing a headwind. . . ." Against the wind, I'm older now,
but still running against the wind." I can readily identify
with the lyrics because when running against a headwind,
I was forced to slow my pace and wait for my physical
reserves to become restored so I could continue to run.
All of us, at sometime on our path of life, will feel we're
running against the wind, when we are struggling to make
it through a valley of our life. Jesus, our Lord and Savior,
has told us that He is always with us, and this means we
can count on Him to be there with us as we struggle to
make it through the valleys of our life. During these valleys we need to pray to Jesus for strength and guidance,
praise Him for His greatness, and then wait, wait upon
the Lord for our spiritual, emotional, and mental reserves
to be restored. "But they that wait upon the Lord shall
renew their strength. They shall mount up with wings as
eagles. They shall run and not grow weary. They shall
walk and not faint" (Isa. 40:31, KJV).

In the midst of a valley it is easy to feel alone, believing that we alone have to do all the struggling to overcome our difficulty. If we believe there is a chance that
we may die, the feelings of isolation and aloneness are
ever present, even in the midst of those who care for us,
and these feelings can overwhelm us if we allow them. I
believe if we are facing a serious disease or even our own
death, we are acutely aware that this is one journey we
alone have to take. No one can go through it for us. Those
who have a spiritual anchor can draw upon their faith to
sustain them in their struggle. It must be scary for those
without this faith. Even those of us with a spiritual anchor can feel, at times, overwhelmed and wonder if God
has left us.

In the tiny booklet, *You Are Not Alone,* published by
Unity School Of Christianity (Unity Village, Missouri),

James Dillet Freeman authored a brief segment entitled, "You Are Not Alone." He makes the reader acutely aware that we can develop a sense that God is always with us. He states:

> God is with you. You do not have to face your problems alone. You do not have to make your overcomings alone. There is One with you always who will help you in everything you have to meet. You may feel; however, that you have no awareness that God is with you. If that is so, you can develop it. You can develop it through prayer. It may come immediately. It may come slowly. But if you consciously and persistently seek the presence of God, you will find that presence.
>
> Regular periods of prayer are helpful if you have the time and the desire for them; but best of all, throughout the day remind yourself that God is with you. Especially the first thing on waking and the last thing before falling asleep, remind yourself that God is with you. Whenever something comes up, whenever you feel that you need strength or freedom or wisdom or peace, remind yourself that God is with you, helping you.
>
> In this way you will come to know that truly God *is* with you. You will come to feel His loving, living presence. God is Spirit. He is intelligence, love, life. And you will feel His presence as a quickening of your intelligence, love, and life. You will feel Him as a new sense of assurance and peace such as you never had before. You will feel Him as new vitality and strength.
>
> God is with you! That is the truth. Keep it before you. Think it, affirm it, repeat it until you have fixed it indelibly in your mind and heart, until you feel it in the inmost fiber of your being. You

will feel it. Be sure of that. You will feel it so clearly that you will never doubt it again. Then nothing you have to meet will ever seem overpowering again, for you will know that with you is something infinitely more powerful, something braver than any fear, stronger than any weakness, firmer than any wavering, wiser than any doubt. You will know that in you is the divine capacity to meet every situation, the wisdom to know what should be done, the strength to do it. You will know that with you is God, and you will never be alone again. (pgs., 3-5, 8)

God is with you.

One of my favorite Bible stories (John 11) is where Jesus raises Lazarus from the dead. Jesus was a close friend to Lazarus and his two sisters, Mary and Martha. When Jesus received a message from Mary and Martha saying that their brother was very ill, Jesus waited two more days before going to Bethany to be with them. He waited so the glory of God could be manifested. When Jesus arrived at Bethany, Mary came to Him and ". . . she fell down at his feet, saying, 'Sir, if you had been here, my brother would still be alive.' Mary was weeping and Jesus was greatly moved, bringing tears to his eyes."

> When confronted with the loss of his dear friend and the emotions of those around him, Jesus wept. Even though Jesus knew that he was the resurrection and that he would bring Lazarus back to life, Jesus still cried.
>
> His example teaches something important: God hears our cries of despair. God sees our grief and cries with us. Even though God knows that the resurrection will come, God understands our loss and is present to cry along with us and comfort us. (Michael Cline, pg., 9)

The Upper Room (Daily Devotional Guide) for 5 July 1999.

Jesus is with us in our grief and valleys of life. He feels the same pain we do, and He is there to comfort us and guide us through the pain if we will let Him.

Compared to eternity, we are on this earth but a blink of an eye, a minuscule amount of time. It seems much of our early life, even into middle age, we are caught up with attaining the education and skills we need for successful employment, getting married and raising kids, trying to make a living, and pursuing self pleasure and materialism with few, if any, thoughts of trying to understand our purpose here on earth.

I feel I have had plenty of bumps on my road of life, sometimes even boulders with which to contend and you, no doubt, have had plenty of trials yourself. "Thank you God for these trials for they are opportunities for us to grow and with growth, we are drawn closer to you." If our growth leads us to believe that Christ is our Lord and Savior, that He died on the cross so that we might be saved, and by God's grace, then we can look forward to the glory of God and living eternally in Heaven.

> Yet this short time of distress will result in God's richest blessing upon us forever and ever! So we do not look at what we can see right now, the troubles all around us, but we look forward to the joys in heaven which we have not yet seen. The troubles will soon be over, but the joys to come will last forever." (2 Cor. 4:17-18)

In his book, *Guide to Stress Reduction*, L. John Mason stated:

> Take care of yourself, and feel good about yourself. I can remember painful times in my own life during which I was confused, hurt, and unable to make any decisions. I had not yet discovered stress

reduction and was blindly searching for something to stabilize my life. I would not want to relive these periods in my life—but I would not want to give them up either—because I learned and experienced so much from this chaos and turmoil. I believe most people learn and grow—not when everything is going well in their lives—but when they are experiencing difficulty and pain and have to change. Growth and change are not always easy or fun, but they are a necessary part of being alive. (pgs., 164-165)

Many years ago I read a small paperback book, *Prison to Praise* by Merlin Carothers. He tells of how God came into his life. He was a young man in the army which did not suit him too well. He was once court-martialled and put in the army prison (brig). After his release from the army, he was visiting his grandparents, and they wanted him to go to evening church services with them. He did not want to do this, but could not think of a way to get out of it, so reluctantly, he went with them to church. While there, Merlin had a moving spiritual experience which changed his life forever. Later, he went to seminary school and reenlisted in the military as a chaplin. He has written numerous praise books; *Power in Praise, Praise Works, Answers to Praise*, etc.

Young army men and women would bring their problems to Chaplin Carothers, looking for assistance, support, and solutions. His books are replete with examples where he used praise, supported by Bible verses, with those seeking his help. Initially, his clients often expressed to Chaplin Carothers, "How can I be thankful for this difficult situation I am in?" Chaplin Carothers utilized Bible verses to support his belief that we need to trust God and praise Him for all things.

"Trust in the Lord with all your heart and lean not on your own understanding; in all your ways acknowledge him, and he will make your paths straight" (Prov. 3:5-6, NIV).

"Rejoice always, pray without ceasing, give thanks in all circumstances; for this is the will of God in Christ Jesus for you" (1 Thess. 5:16-18, RSV).

"And we know that all that happens to us is working for our good if we love God and are fitting into his plans" (Rom. 8:28).

"God's purpose in this was that we should praise God and give glory to him for doing these mighty things for us, who were the first to trust in Christ" (Eph. 1:12).

"Be delighted with the Lord. Then he will give you all your heart's desires" (Ps. 37:4).

Reverend Carothers wrote in *Power in Praise*, "Any form of sincere prayers opens the door for God's power to move into our lives. But the prayer of praise releases more of God's power than any other form of petition. The Bible gives examples which demonstrate this fact again and again" (pg. 12).

"It is through gratitude that we become aware of the presence of God. God is working in your life. You are not alone. The whole of the universe is working together."

"We live on the earth; we breathe the same air. Be grateful and you will feel the connection."

"When you are grateful, you will come to love yourself and all that you are. When you are grateful for where you've been and what you've done, you are at peace - with yourself and your family. And that, my friend, is the perfect legacy, the very best gift you can give to the future generation" (pg., 137). (Excerpted from *Wonderful Ways to Love a Grandchild* by Judy Ford, copyright 1997, used by permission of Conari Press.)

In the book, *Death: The Final Stage of Growth*, by Elizabeth Kubler-Ross, a funeral director and his wife, Roy and Jane Nichols, wrote the chapter, "Funerals: A Time for Grief and Growth." They wrote, "The most beautiful people we have known are those who have known defeat, known suffering, known struggle, known loss, and have found their way out of the depths. These persons have an appreciation, a sensitivity, and an understanding of life that fills them with compassion, gentleness, and a deep loving concern. Beautiful people do not just happen" (pg., 96).

The defeats, sufferings, trials, and losses that we each encounter on our life's path provide us with the opportunity to grow into a beautiful person with depth of character, a person filled with compassion, gentleness, and loving concern. However, we do not always perceive these tribulations as an opportunity for growth. When we are emotionally and mentally distraught over a difficult situation in which we are confronted, too often we make poor choices to rid ourself of painful feelings and mental anguish. In this type of situation, we tend to make choices which hurt ourselves and/or others. We may turn to alcohol, drugs (illegal and/or prescription), sexual affairs, overeating, depression, and various forms of abuse to ourselves and others in an effort to dull our feelings or to get rid of our frustration and anger, so that we experience less emotional pain, at least temporarily.

If we wrestle with our emotional and mental pain in a rational and responsible way, and perceive the difficult situation as an opportunity for emotional, mental, and spiritual growth, we will grow in a positive direction. Also, viewing challenging situations in our life as an opportunity for growth promotes a very positive attitude within us. Merlin Carothers believes that looking for the good in all situations in our life opens the door for the power of Holy Spirit to work in our lives, assisting us in growing and managing the painful situation. Perceiving situations in a negative manner tends to reduce the likelihood for God's power to work in our life.

Even though it would not have been my choice to have lymphatic cancer, I see numerous benefits about it for which to be thankful. I can genuinely praise God for the following:

1. This book would not have been written without it.
2. I have had a great increase in opportunities to witness my faith in Christ.
3. It is very unlikely that I would have known of the many angel stories about which I have read and which people have shared directly with me, stories which have given me great hope and reassurance.
4. It has drawn me closer to God, making me more aware of His presence.
5. It has made me acutely aware that I need to be a channel through which God can touch the lives of those around me in a positive and spiritual way.
6. It has forced me to put my trust fully in God, which He has always wanted me to do.

Another benefit from a having a serious, life-threatening, health condition is that it is a great antidote to vanity. As we age and/or face a serious illness we are provided the opportunity for reassessing our life and our values, and to be enlightened by what really is important in life.

There have been many days since being diagnosed with a ruptured appendix (June 1992) and, later, non-Hodgkins low-grade lymphoma cancer (Aug. 1992) when the value of material items had no meaning to me. These deep valleys are a great opportunity for us to develop a more accurate perception of what has worth (spiritual - fruit of the Holy Spirit) and what matters little. Since being first diagnosed with cancer, I perceive that I am now on the back side of the mountain and that it is okay. Keeping life simple is growing increasingly important to me. Seeking too many material things or having a complex life style is detrimental to hearing the still small voice of the Holy Spirit within us.

In education we talk about the "teachable moment." It is the moment when the child is mentally focused and receptive, emotionally calm, and has sufficient background knowledge or experiences that will allow him/her to fully grasp the new concept or material that is being presented. Unfortunately in education, too often the teacher does not find the student in this state. Many students come into the classroom with emotional baggage which interferes with them being at the optimum state for learning. Their emotional baggage comes from homes where their parents are divorced, single, blended families, or there are financial stressors, alcoholism, illegal drug usage, and various forms of abuse (emotional, physical, and sexual).

But there is also a spiritual, teachable moment, a time when a person is most receptive to hearing the message of Jesus and spiritual salvation. I believe a person is most receptive to hearing this spiritual message, not when things are going smoothly in his or her life, but when he or she is experiencing pain (emotional, mental, or physical) sufficient enough to want relief. Reaching out to God is more likely to happen when we are feeling deep pain, assuming the person chooses not to use means destructive to himself and/or others in an effort to reduce or eliminate the pain. It may happen at a funeral of someone whom we deeply care about, or upon seeing our child, spouse, relative, or close friend face a serious crisis or even terminal illness. I believe there is a high probability that if we, ourselves, are facing a crisis, that we will call out in our pain to God. God will hear our call!

Call unto me, and I will answer thee, and shew thee great and mighty things, which thou knowest not. (Jer. 33:3, KJV)

Blessed are those who mourn, for they shall be comforted. (Matt. 5:4, RSV)

In my distress I called to the Lord; I cried to my God for help. From his temple he heard my voice; my cry came before him, into his ears. (Ps. 18:6, NIV)

Even though I walk through the valley of the shadow of death; I fear no evil; for thou art with me; thy rod and staff, they comfort me. (Ps. 23:4, RSV)

Though the mountains be shaken and the hills be removed, yet my unfailing love for you will not be shaken nor my covenant of peace be removed," says the Lord, "who has compassion on you. (Isa. 54:10, NIV)

The Lord is . . . my God, my rock, in whom I take refuge, my shield, and the {home} of my salvation, {and} my stronghold. (Ps. 18:2, RSV)

For I am certain that nothing . . . in all creation . . . will be able to separate us from the love of God which is ours through Christ Jesus our Lord. (Rom. 8:38, TEV)

Be strong and of good courage; be not frightened, neither be dismayed; for the LORD your God is with you wherever you go. (Josh. 1:9, RSV)

"Thank you God for these spiritual, teachable moments in our life when we choose to bring our emotional and mental pain to you, knowing that you are always there for us, to comfort us with peace and unconditional love that is beyond our earthly comprehension."

Viktor Frankl, in his book, *Man's Search for Meaning,* tells of the terrible conditions during WW II when he was a prisoner in the German concentration Camp at Auschwitz, and he was later transferred to a camp affili- ated with Dachau. As a Jewish psychiatrist, he was often called upon to speak to fellow prisoners in his dark, cold, and over crowded building, to say the words which gave them hope and encouragement. Tears flowed freely from the men as he spoke with deeply moving words of com- fort and hope. Mr. Frankl wrote notes on tiny scraps of paper which he hoped to use in writing a book if he was to survive the inhumane conditions. He wrote of how he could tell when a prisoner had given up, had lost all hope, and was ready to die. He noted that one's chance of sur- vival in a concentration camp was one in twenty-eight. He himself came close to giving up all hope of surviving.

Mr. Frankl noted that even in the horrendous con- ditions of life in a concentration camp, an individual still had many choices before him each hour of the day:

> The experiences of camp life show that man does have a choice of action. There were enough ex- amples, often of a heroic nature, which proved that apathy could be overcome, irritability sup- pressed. Man *can* preserve a vestige of spiritual freedom, of independence of mind, even in such terrible conditions of psychic and physical stress.

> We who lived in concentration camps can remem- ber the men who walked through the huts com- forting others, giving away their last piece of bread. They may have been few in number, but they offer sufficient proof that everything can be taken from a man but one thing; the last of the human freedoms—to choose one's attitude in any given set of circumstances, to choose one's own way . . . in the final analysis it becomes clear that

the sort of person a prisoner became was the result of an inner decision, and not the result of camp influences alone. Fundamentally, therefore, any man can, even under such circumstances, decide what shall become of him—mentally and spiritually. He may retain his human dignity even in a concentration camp. (pgs., 103-105)

And each of us will choose the attitude with which we face our valleys of life and our own death. Having a strong, spiritual anchor provides the strength to help us weather the pain and discomfort that we may experience as we go through our valleys of life and even the process of watching our bodies physically die. The attitude with which we handle our own death can not only help preserve our sense of dignity, but can be reassuring to loved ones who are there with us, watching us make our transition into the spiritual world where great unconditional love, peace, and joy awaits us, if we trust Jesus as our Lord and Savior.

In life we can expect to face challenges, trials, losses, and pain. We may, at times, wonder why life has to be so painful and so difficult. For some, life becomes too much to bear, and they take their own life.

Viktor Frankl wrote:

Dostoevski said once, "There is only one thing that I dread: not to be worthy of my sufferings." These words frequently came to my mind after I became acquainted with those martyrs whose behavior in camp, whose suffering and death, bore witness to the fact that the last inner freedom cannot be lost. It can be said that they were worthy of their sufferings; the way they bore their suffering was a genuine inner achievement. It is this spiritual freedom—which cannot be taken away—that makes life meaningful and purposeful. If there is a meaning in life at all, then there must be a meaning in suffering. Suffering is an ineradicable part of life, even as fate and death. Without suffering and death human life cannot be complete. (pgs., 105-106)

The way in which a man accepts his fate and all the suffering it entails, the way in which he takes up his cross, gives him ample opportunity—even under the most difficult circumstances—to add a deeper meaning to his life. It may remain brave, dignified and unselfish. Or in the bitter fight for self-preservation he may forget his human dignity and become no more than an animal. Here lies the chance for a man either to make use of or to forego the opportunities of attaining the values that a difficult situation may afford him. And this decides whether he is worthy of his sufferings or not. (pgs., 106-107)

Of the prisoners only a few kept their full inner liberty and obtained those values which their suffering afforded, but even one such example is sufficient proof that man's inner strength may raise him above his outward fate. Such men are not only in concentration camps. Everywhere man is confronted with fate, with the chance of achieving something through his own suffering. (pg., 107)

For what matters above all is the attitude we take toward suffering, the attitude in which we take our suffering upon ourselves. Suffering ceases to be suffering in some way at the moment it finds meaning, such as the meaning of a sacrifice . . . that man's main concern is not to gain pleasure or to avoid pain, but rather to see a meaning in his life. That is why man is even ready to suffer, on the condition, to be sure, that his suffering has a meaning. (pgs., 178-179)

We have all heard or read stories of single parents, usually women, who, with little money or education, worked for years at multiple jobs to provide their children with food, shelter, and loving care. Often times these parents continued their arduous work for years in an effort to help pay their children's way through college. You can be sure a parent of this type saw meaning in their suffering and they were willing to go to great depths in an effort to sacrifice their life for the benefit of their children. And along the way, this type of parent had a great opportunity to develop tremendous character.

> Dear brothers, is your life full of difficulties and temptations? Then be happy, for when the way is rough, your patience has a chance to grow. So let it grow, and don't try to squirm out of your problems. For when your patience is finally in full bloom, then you will be ready for anything, strong in character, full and complete. (James 1:2-4)

Mr. Frankl continued in his book, "There are situations in which one is cut off from the opportunity to do one's work or to enjoy one's life, but what never can be ruled out is the unavoidability of suffering. In accepting this challenge to suffer bravely, life has a meaning up to the last moment, and it retains this meaning literally to the end" (pg., 181).

When life becomes stressful or I find myself in a valley, I often turn to nature for solace and serenity. It is a time when I dwell on spiritual matters, sing hymns, and attempt to be fully receptive to the presence and love of God. I seek guidance from God, for any message He may want to communicate with me which will assist me on my spiritual path. I believe for many of us who enjoy being in the beauty and wonder of nature, we are afforded the opportunity to feel a closeness to God, rejuvenating us in the process.

During the summer months in Wyoming I have a favorite place where I go to immerse myself fully in the natural beauty of nature, Elkhart Park in Bridger National Forest in the Wind River Mountain Range.

Visible at the trailhead is snow and ice lingering in the valleys of the bare mountain peaks miles away. I begin traversing down the meandering, worn path to Long Lake, two miles all downhill. The wind is swishing through the tops of the many tall pines. The morning mountain air is cool and invigorating to my body, making me feel alive, as the summer sun is slowly making its way upward and through the abundant trees. Along the way little chipmunks, with their cute little stripes on their back, dart and scurry from spot to spot, always keeping me within their sight. Squirrels chatter noisily, signaling an intruder, as they scamper about in the many, tall pines. A grouse moseys slowly through the bushes and tall grass within a few feet of the trail, seemingly unconcerned of my footsteps close by on the dusty, rocky path. I hear a tiny mountain stream nearby as it makes its way to a distant lake far below. Huckleberry plants abound along the trail, and I consume many of these tiny tasty morsels. Mountain flowers stand proud in the gentle, caressing breeze. Birds give forth their melodious songs, greeting the new day with joy.

My thoughts turn to God and spiritual matters. Prayer and angel experiences, Bible verses, and spiritual affirmations come to mind in my desire to feel a closeness to God and His beautiful world. I think of my health, wondering how it is all going to turn out and know I will put my trust in God. I praise God for his plan for me, feeling the joy and unconditional love God must have for me if he cares enough about me to have a plan which I am to follow. Prayers are said for relatives and friends who are in need of spiritual support. I seek an open mind so as to allow space for thoughts that may be God inspired. I relish and absorb the tranquility and natural beauty that surrounds me as I continue my journey on the downward, crooked path.

Long Lake lies before me as I approach the top of a small ridge. It glistens with beauty from the light of the morning sun which has risen over the rugged, mountain peaks. I sit quietly on a long, old, barren, pine log as it lays pointing toward the lake on the inner side of the ridge. The rays of the warm sun touch my tanned skin and warm my body to its inner being. Great calm and contentment flow over me as if wrapped in a soft, warm blanket. Three, young muskrats, appearing unaware of my nearby presence, playfully chase each other in and around a large, hollowed-out log, partially submerged in the cool, clear water. In the distance, two ducks weave and bob along on the smooth, peaceful water. I think of Psalm 23 (KJV). *"The Lord is my Shepherd. I shall not want. He maketh me to lie down in green pastures. He leadeth me beside the still waters. He restoreth my soul. . . ."* Beauty and peace calms my spirit and restores my soul. I feel centered and at peace. My world seems in balance. "Thank you Lord!" *"My heart is tuned to the quietness that the stillness of nature inspires"* (Nature Meditations, pg., 160).

Walking slowly and quietly along the shore, I hold my frequent glances at the lake, reluctant to let go of the serenity and beauty it possesses. Shortly, I climb to the top of a large, rounded, rocky bluff where I rest in some shade and refresh myself. I feel the warmth of the rock, heated by the late-morning sun. Thirty feet below, white water gushes noisily through a narrow, rocky channel as it flows swiftly out of Long Lake and on down the narrow stream. I immerse myself in the delightful sights and sounds which surround me, allowing the experience to permeate the depth of my being. I leisurely consume my grapes, snicker doodles, and soft drink as I feel a oneness with the beauty and tranquility of nature. Later, as I munch on walnuts and almonds, I contemplate leaving the warmth and serenity of this safe haven.

Leaving the area, my eyes and ears no longer provide my senses with the beauty, peace, and stillness which enveloped me while I rested at one of my favorite spots in nature. But my memory continues to provide me with visualizations and deep thoughts of the specialness of the experience. I can recall it anytime I desire, reliving my serene unity with nature. It will be invaluable in helping me get through my valleys of life.

Not only can nature provide us with feelings of serenity, inner calm, quietness, and a oneness, but it can help us heal our inner being. It can provide us with strength to meet the challenges which each of us encounter on our life's journey.

The following, as written in Joseph Cornell's book, *Listening to Nature*:

> "Walk away quietly in any
> direction and taste the
> freedom of the mountaineer. . . .
>
> Climb the mountains and get their
> tidings. Nature's
> peace will flow into you as
> sunshine flows into
> trees. The winds will blow their
> own freshness into
> you, and the storms their energy,
> while cares will drop
> off like autumn leaves."
>
> —John Muir
> (Son of the Wilderness , pg., 176)

With beauty before me,
May I walk
With beauty behind me,
May I walk
With beauty above me,
May I walk
With beauty below me,
May I walk
With beauty all around me,
May I walk
Wandering on a trail of beauty,
Lively, I walk.

—Navajo Indians

None of us would choose the valleys of our life, but we can all expect to encounter them at some point on our life's journey. These valleys are a great opportunity for us to grow emotionally, mentally, and spiritually. If this growth brings us closer to our Lord and Savior Jesus Christ, then this is something for which to give thanks to God. If we have a spiritual anchor we will be able, regardless of the emotional, mental, and/or physical pain, to weather the storm. If we lack a sufficient spiritual anchor, we are likely to make choices which are detrimental to ourselves or others.

"Heavenly Father, thank you for the valleys of my life, those times when I struggled to meet the challenge of the trial before me. Too often I have tried to rely totally upon myself, not fully appreciating that you were always there to help me if I were to ask. With the return of the lymphoma, I am in the midst of another valley. As barnacles adhere tightly to a great and mighty ship, my faith will adhere to you Lord, my rock and salvation. I will put my trust and hope in you, and we'll go forth together . . . rejoicing."

If you want favor with both God and man, and a reputation for good judgment and common sense, then trust the Lord completely; don't ever trust yourself. In everything you do, put God first, and he will direct you and crown your efforts with success. (Prov. 3:4-6)

This I declare, that he alone is my refuge, my place of safety; he is my God, and I am trusting him. (Ps. 91:2)

My soul claims the Lord as my inheritance; therefore I will hope in him. The Lord is wonderfully good to those who wait for him, to those who seek for him. It is good both to hope and wait quietly for the salvation of the Lord. (Lam. 3:24-26)

V

Angel Encounters

*"Do not forget to entertain strangers for by so doing some
. . . have entertained angels without knowing it."*

—Hebrews 13:2, NIV

*"You are about to embark on an adventure
with the angels. Your passport is an open heart—and
we suggest you travel light."*

—Alma Daniel
(American Psychotherapist)

My daughter Donna gave me a book for Father's
Day 1994, and I suspect that God may have guided her
to select that book for me. It was, *Where Angels Walk,* by
Joan Wester Anderson. It has many brief stories about
individuals' encounters with angels. I found it delightful
reading as well as reassuring. As a result of the joy I found
in reading the angel stories, I have given away many copies
of this book. Usually a thought comes to me that I need
to buy another book for a certain person. Sometimes that
person or someone they love or care about is facing a
difficult situation themselves. I have also given copies to
people who seem to have a special, spiritual quality about
them or depth of character. Twice, after giving this book
to someone, they or a loved one has shared an angel experience with me.

I gave one copy of *Where Angels Walk* to Brenda. The first time I met her it was readily apparent that she was a compassionate, honest, and caring woman. Brenda and my son Scott were in some of the same law enforcement classes at Weber State University in Ogden, Utah. They became good friends and were supportive of each other. Brenda lives on a few acres, between Ogden and Salt Lake City, with her two children and several horses. Scott is very fond of horses so he helped Brenda with construction work on her small barn, cleaning, and grooming her horses, etc. Brenda invited me to ride with her and Scott when I came to visit him in Ogden. The three of us went riding on two occasions, and she impressed me with her quality values, compassion, and depth of character. I admired the friendship and support she and Scott had for each other. I decided at that time I would give her a copy of the book. I sent a copy to Scott, who in turn, gave Brenda the book. I received a delightful thank you letter from Brenda, and she wrote about an angel experience she had when she was a young girl. This was her angel experience:

An Angel to Comfort Me

When I was a child of 6 or 7 years, I became very ill. I hadn't remembered ever feeling as ill as I did this particular evening. My mother endlessly tended to my needs, as she placed a cold wet washcloth on my forehead, took my temperature, and prepared some tea which I slowly sipped. My bedroom was lit only by the light from the hall. My mother had left my side for a few minutes to use the bathroom. As soon as she shut the bathroom door, a young woman with a gentle face appeared at the foot of my bed. At first, I was frightened because the stranger appeared so sud-

Marie
(granddaughter)

denly, out of nowhere. I inquired, "Mommy?" The stranger did not respond, but instead bent down and picked up my doll at the foot of my bed and cradled it in her arms. I saw my doll so clearly in her gentle arms, yet when I looked at the foot of my bed, my doll was still lying right there. As I waited for my mother's return, I did not take my eyes off the stranger. My memory of her is quite clear—even 35 years later. She was quite tall and slender. The long white flowing gown which draped her presence was billowing gently as clouds in a subtle wind. She appeared as though, if I had tried reaching her, my hand would pass directly through her. Even my doll took on a translucent quality as she looked at it with a loving, caring gaze. Suddenly, I felt quite peaceful as I watched her cuddling my doll as though she were real. I realized at that moment that the stranger meant me no harm. She had taken over my mother's duties in my mother's absence. My mother returned and just as quickly, the stranger left my room. I knew I had been looked in on by an angel.

Brenda's mother, whom I never met, died 2 July 1997, of cancer. Brenda said she had been very health conscious, as I have, with regard to exercise and diet. With a short time to live, Hospice was involved in meeting her needs. One day when the Hospice nurse came to see her, Brenda's mother had a spiritual experience. Brenda explained it this way:

The Hug

When my mother's doctor realized the chemotherapy was not working, she struggled with her heartfelt condolences to my mother and our family. She then referred my parents to Hospice.

My father had contact with Hospice that following Monday. The first appointment for a home health aide to come to the home was scheduled for that Wednesday. It was initially decided an aide would visit three days weekly—Mondays, Wednesdays, and Fridays. Services would increase as needed.

I visited with my mother on the evening after Doris Valentine had made her first, and quite impressionable, house call.

My mother had been on a lot of a pain medication. However, she was unusually alert and animated as she spoke enthusiastically about her Doris. My mother could not say enough about how much she enjoyed Doris as an individual. She felt they had really clicked.

She then went on to tell me that Doris had played the piano for her. She went on and on about Doris and how she had played "The Rose" beautifully. Mother then told me she had asked Doris to play that same song at her funeral. I asked my mother what Doris' response was to that. My mother told me quite proudly, she said, "She would be honored." My mother was already looking forward to Friday when Doris would be returning. Friday didn't come for my mother—she died that very evening.

Good to her word, Doris did indeed play "The Rose" at the funeral. I then understood the passion my mother was feeling when she described Doris' playing. It was the most beautiful thing I had ever heard.

After the service, Doris had told each of us there was more to the story than we knew about. She told us she would like to speak to all of us (my father, sister, brother, and myself) together after everyone had gone.

Doris told us a shortened (and less emotional under the circumstances) version of her experience with my mother. She felt it would give us some comfort after our loss.

Quite some months later I felt inclined to call Doris and ask her to explain in detail the "hug" she received.

The thing which stuck out in her mind was the fact that when she entered my mother's bedroom, she did not smell death as she has come to know with so many of her hospice patients. She said as she was introduced to my mother by my father, my mother said, "It's very nice to meet you Doris. I see you've brought your son with you." Doris was taken aback as she had no one with her. Doris asked, "Excuse me?" By this time Doris was at my mother's side somewhat crouched down. My mother repeated her statement. Doris said my mother was looking over her shoulder as if she was looking at someone. Doris said she tried to maintain her composure, her professionalism, and not allow herself to get flustered. She knew she was there to care for a patient and perform the necessary duties. In the back of her mind she had many questions.

Once Doris' duties were complete and my mother was comfortable, Doris asked mother's permission to play her grand piano. Doris played "The Rose." When she reentered my mother's bedroom, my mother said, "Now we have a favor to ask you." My father and brother were standing by my mother's bed with tears in their eyes. I can actually hear Doris's heartfelt reply, "I would be honored."

Doris told me she had thought about mother's words again, "I see you've brought your son with you." Doris lost her son, Wesley, (they called him Wes) about six years before my mother died. Wes was diagnosed with Aplastic Anemia. His bone marrow just stopped producing healthy cells. The doctors told them a bone marrow transplant could be a cure for his condition. This would be his "best bet" for a normal life.

After receiving the new marrow from his older brother, his body began rejecting the transplant. It was a long, hard struggle—watching their 11-year-old son endure so much pain. Wes ultimately died of complications from the transplant.

Doris has always wanted some sort of sign that he was there—somewhere. In her line of work, she has heard many accounts of such things. She wanted so badly to ask my mother; what he looked like, how tall he was, etc. She felt she might attain the answers she longed for on her next visit.

There was no next visit. My mother died that same night. Doris would never gain the answers to her questions. I asked Doris if that didn't leave her a bit empty. Her reply to me was, "Not at all. I felt as though I had gotten a great big hug." Doris expressed, "Thanks to your mother's gift, I am at peace."

I feel we all received a gift from Doris' wonderful experience. Thank you so much Doris and mother . . . and Wesley.

Bert was a janitor in one of the schools I work at, Yellowstone Elementary, the first two years I was employed as a school psychologist for this school district. He was retired from the fire department, but since he lived close to the school, he had worked there as a janitor for two years for extra money. In October of 1995, I was told by another janitor (Carol) at Yellowstone that Bert wasn't in very good shape. I bought another copy of the book and took it to his home that same month. He was skin and bones and hooked up to an oxygen tank to ease the damage of too many years of heavy smoking. I shared with him my own health situation and an angel experience of a friend's mother. I told him I thought we were in for quite a spiritual experience when we died, especially if we were spiritually prepared. Bert expressed interest in reading the book. Carol told me his family was hoping he would make it through the Christmas holidays, which gratefully he did. But in mid-January I received a thank you card from his wife which read:

Angels in My Midst

Paul, I am writing you to let you know that Bert read the angel book and he did find the Lord. One week before he died, he told me two angels were in the house with him. The day before he went into his coma, he told me the two angels were at the hospital with him.

Thanks for being a good friend to Bert. Pauline

Wouldn't it have been a delight to have heard their conversation?

I called Pauline to thank her for the card and for sharing Bert's delightful angel experience with me. I asked her specific questions about his experience, but all she could tell me was that Bert said, "Things were going to be all right." Bert wasn't much for doing a lot of talking. I was very pleased and thanked God that Bert had this experience. He must have felt much love, peace, and reassurance in their midst.

His experience made me recall a parable expressed by Jesus:

The owner of an estate went out early one morning to hire workers for his harvest field. He agreed
to pay them $20 a day and sent them out to work.
A couple of hours later he was passing a hiring
hall and saw some men standing around waiting
for jobs, so he sent them also into his fields, telling them he would pay them whatever was right
at the end of the day. At noon and again around
three o'clock in the afternoon he did the same
thing. At five o'clock that evening he was in town
again and saw some more men standing around
and asked them, 'Why haven't you been working
today?' 'Because no one hired us,' they replied.
That evening he told the paymaster to call the
men in and pay them, beginning with the last men
first. The men hired at five o'clock were paid, each
receiving $20. So, when the men hired earlier
came to get their money, they assumed they would
receive much more. But they, too, were paid $20.
(Matt. 20:1-10)

No matter at what time we come to Christ during
our lifetime, we all receive the same grand gift of eternal
life, if and only if, we believe in Christ as our Lord and
Savior, believing that He died for our sins, that He rose
from the dead, and by God's grace we have been saved.
The thank you card from Pauline suggests that Bert came
to Christ very late in his life, but he was entitled to the
same gift as those who come to Christ at an early age.
There is danger, however, in waiting, for we may miss
this all important opportunity.

Trudi Werner was the librarian who worked in two
schools where I also worked as the school psychologist.
Her husband, Dr. Michael Werner, was the gifted surgeon who operated on me when I had the ruptured appendix. About two years after he operated on me, he was
diagnosed with a malignant, brain tumor. Trudi and Mike

traveled to Japan where he was given a radiation treatment which was not available to him in the United States. They returned home with the knowledge that his life expectancy was only a few years. While he was recuperating at home, Dr. Werner, who was an avid hunter and nature lover, began having seizures while riding his ATV (all terrain vehicle) over the rough Wyoming terrain. These reoccurring seizures eventually led to his death. Dr. Werner's children took their father's death very hard, and Trudi felt she needed to move the family to another state. During this long ordeal, Trudi's mother Vivian had been living with the Werner family. I was fortunate to talk to Vivian a couple of times on the phone during Dr. Werner's illness, but I never met her in person. She had been a school teacher in her younger years.

Before Trudi moved with her family, we exchanged addresses and phone numbers. In October of 1994, I received a message that Vivian had an angel experience a couple of days before she died. Trudi asked in the message that I call her since she had lost my phone number. With exciting anticipation, I called her that same evening. This was the story she told me about her mother's angel experience:

"I'll Be Going with Them Today"

It's hard to know where to begin this description of what happened to my mother, Vivian Vasold, because the appearance of her angels was just part of the continuing flow of her life. I have decided to back up to earlier years to try to help explain her life and why I think the angels came. Mom grew up in a small town in Iowa, raised by Grandmother Pierce and Aunt Gertrude. Her mother died when mom was five years old, and her father didn't feel he could do a good job single parenting, so he left mom with the others. Aunt Gertrude spent her entire life studying the Bible. She and Grandmother Pierce also spent time showing mom how to live a Christian life, a lesson mom carried forward until the day she died.

My mother's idea of a Christian life was straight forward; she prayed every night, never gossiped, and never judged others. She was always gracious and thoroughly enjoyed meeting others. Basically, she lived the Golden Rule—'Do unto others as you would have them do unto you.' When I was young, she would tell me, "People in glass houses shouldn't throw stones." It took me a long time to understand how seriously she believed that. She never made negative comments. When faced with someone's negative action, the worst she would say was "I don't understand why he would do that."

In the fall of 1993 my husband was diagnosed with a brain tumor at the same time that my mother happened to be visiting us from Michigan. She had been a widow for two years, so she decided that she could stay with us and help. When my husband and I went to Japan for treatment of the cancer, she stayed at our home in Wyoming with our three teenagers and "held down the fort." She was 86 at the time. The family did well in our absence, and after returning from Japan we all settled in together.

As my husband's disease progressed, I could see that mom was losing weight. She also developed a dry cough. One day at lunch my husband, Mike, said to mom, "Well Vivian, I wonder which one of us will go first." Mom immediately replied, "It won't be me because I have to take care of Trudi." This indeed proved to be correct. Mike passed away on 21 September 1994. One day after the funeral I took mom to the doctor to see about her cough, and he made the diagnosis of lung cancer. There was no treatment for her because of her frail health. By that time she was surviving on one half of one lung.

Mom, two of my teenage children, and I moved to Colorado in December to be close to our oldest son who was attending college there, leaving one son who was a high school senior behind. One day shortly after settling into our new home in Colorado my mother expressed doubts about life after death. She said she just wasn't sure. I think mom wanted scientific proof. She was well educated and a teacher by profession. She trusted science and kept us informed daily about what she had learned on the Discovery Channel. Her last minute doubts scared me because I knew she was slowly deteriorating.

I finally realized that I had the answer she needed. During my lifetime I have had several ESP experiences that mom knew about. Also, she had read about the predictions of Nostradamus. It suddenly hit me that life is a continuum and that there could be no clairvoyance or ESP if life wasn't a continuum because nothing would happen until the cells divide, until that second in history. It would be impossible to look into the future because it wouldn't exist. When I shared this with her I could see she agreed. One week later mom's angels came.

Our household had settled into a routine. Every morning I would get up and get the kids moving. After driving them to school, I would return home, and then mom and I would have breakfast together. One Monday morning in February, when I got, up I could see that mom had her light on and was sitting up on the side of her bed. When I went into her room and asked her what was wrong, she said, "I have had visitors, and they said that I will be going with them today." I asked her if they had frightened her, and she said no. She said they had prayed together and that there was a beautiful choir. I asked her about them. She said there was a redheaded man and a woman. I told her they were angels. She said if she had to go today, then she would.

Mom said that the angels had left. Later, mom said that the woman was back in her room. When Karla , my daughter, heard her say that, she immediately ran into her room, but she could not see anyone. Finally both people left her room.

That morning I immediately called Rock Springs High School where our son, Kurt, was a senior and told him what had happened. I had him excused from school, and he got on the road to drive the 315 mile trip home. From the time she told me about her visitors until the time my son arrived from Wyoming, mom literally deflated until she looked like a balloon after the air was let out. By afternoon she couldn't sit up nor eat much. The visiting hospice nurse, who had been seeing mom regularly, told us of others who had had similar experiences.

Mom wanted to say good-bye to everyone. As it turned out, she had three days to say her good-byes. She talked to my children, my brother and niece, her sister, and many friends. During these three days she also talked to me. She spent time evaluating her life. She told me that she had only one regret. When she was a young teacher, she retained a girl in sixth grade. Mom just never felt good about this decision and wasn't sure that it had been the best thing for the girl. She said she would soon find out if this had been the right thing to do or not. After listening to her, I asked if she had tried to do her best. She said, "Yes, I have always tried to do my best." That's all any of us can do, our best.

Another time she told me that the children and I would be fine. I wanted to ask her if the angels had told her that, but I didn't. She also said that dying was an interesting experience. One time she cried out, "I'm going, I'm going." A moment later she said, "I guess I'm not."

By Thursday morning mom had greatly deteriorated. When the hospice nurse arrived, she couldn't get a pulse because mom's heart was too weak. However, mom was still alert. She was lying on her back, looking up above the window. She had one hand on her chest and seemed to be trying to bring her other hand up. The hospice nurse saw this and asked, "Vivian, are the angels back?" Mom nodded her head, "Yes." In a short time, she was gone.

It's hard to believe that the death of one so loved could also be so reassuring and comforting to my family and me. My husband had said before he died, "All you have to do is open up your heart, and let Jesus come in." His words and mom's angels have carried us through the dark time of grieving and loss. We are all right; and we are loved. Mom was right. We will be fine.

I found Trudi's mother's angel story delightful and reassuring. A month or so after Trudi had shared this with me, my curiosity got the better of me. I felt I needed to call her again to get answers to questions which plagued me. I wanted to know if the angels/visitors rang the doorbell or did they just appear in her room and did they appear as physical beings? Trudi said that her mother slept with her bedroom door open and that they just appeared in the doorway. They appeared as physical beings, at least initially. Trudi noted that her mother was not particularly a religious person, but she was a spiritual person. From Trudi's description of her mother, I got the impression that Vivian was a very compassionate person who was very accepting of others. She saw the good in others, never judging them.

Betty Saner's husband died in 1985. A week or two later Betty, with her 5-year-old daughter, moved from the place they were living into an apartment. This is her story:

My Husband, The Angel

I had just lost my husband and then I found out that my father had to have a five bypass heart surgery to save his life. It seemed things were happening so fast. I am very close to my father so I began asking God, "Why me?" and at the same time, "Why was he doing this to me?" I felt that the whole world was coming down on me.

My little girl and I were so busy trying to get the new apartment in shape, and we were tired. I put her to bed and then I went in and made sure the front door was locked and chained. I sat down for a few minutes then decided that I needed to go to bed too. I was lying there resting during this cold, January night, and I kept feeling so cold that I thought that I didn't have the heater on, so I got up to check it and it was on. I went back to bed and as I was lying there I still felt cold when I saw a light. Thinking it was my daughter who had gotten up, I went to her bedroom to check on her. She was sound asleep. I went back to bed, and by now I was really shivering. There was a white light in the hallway, and as I looked, I saw something moving. I thought it was my little girl. The light and movement came closer to me. I was scared so I pulled the covers up over my head. As I eased the covers down, I saw my husband standing over my bed looking at me. He said to me, "Don't worry, I am okay. I am with grandpa and with Pete's dad." I was so scared that I pulled the covers over my head and laid there for a few minutes. Shortly, I moved the covers down and he was gone. I could feel cold air, and I got up to check once again on the door and my little girl. My daughter was okay and still asleep in her bed. When I went to the front room, I found that the door was open and the chain was still locked. I had boxes in front of the door too. They were still in place, but the door was opened and chained. I told my family about my husband coming to check on us and that he told me he was okay and not to worry about him as he is with his grandfather and a good friend of the family. I never saw him after that night. It was just him making sure that we were okay and assuring me that he was okay too.

Wade Jensen was a 10-year-old boy when he saw his first angel. This is his story.

Grandmother's Reassurance

Sometime after my grandfather was killed in an automobile accident I was sleeping with my grandmother upstairs at my parent's home. I awoke and looked toward the side of the bed my grandmother was sleeping on and saw my perception of what an angel should look like (a white glowing figure in a robe) bent over my grandmother as if he was telling her something. At the

time, and to this day, I believe he was comforting
her, telling her grandpa was all right and that everything would be okay. I soon fell asleep and have
not had an experience like this since.

I believe that God has given angels the power to appear as physical beings when the occasion warrants it. I
suspect many of us have encountered angels in human
form, but did not recognize them as such, especially if
we were not spiritually tuned.

I have not experienced angels as told in these stories,
but I may very well have encountered an angel that appeared in human form. During the summer of 1996, I
decided, since it was a beautiful sunny day, to walk a mile
or so to the grocery store to purchase a few items.

I had just walked a short distance onto the far corner
of the huge grocery store parking lot when a young man
nearby approached me. It seemed strange that I had not
noticed him until that moment, even though there was
enormous space all around. He asked for some money to
get to his destination, which he said was Ogden, Utah.
His destination caught my attention right away since my
son Scott lived there. He said he was from Oklahoma,
which meant he had traveled at least a thousand miles
already. For someone to have traveled that far with little
money, you would expect that they would look tired from
having taken short naps in their vehicle, have wrinkled
clothing, and for a man, be unshaven. However, this was
not the case as the young man was well groomed, had a
neat appearance, and was clean-shaven. He appeared as
a man who had just gotten dressed and walked out of his
home.

He said his vehicle was in the K-Mart parking lot,
which was not far away, but blocked from my view by a
service station. I asked him if he had gone to the police
or any church, believing they would provide him with
help or send him to an agency which is known to assist

travelers in similar situations. He responded that he had not. I suggested we go into the grocery store to see what we might find in the way of help. I thought the service desk in the grocery store would call the police or that they would know of a church or agency to contact to assist the young man.

I started walking in the direction of the grocery store, thinking that he was following me. After ten or fifteen steps I turned to see if he was behind me and he was nowhere in sight. He could have walked fifty feet in any direction from where we had been standing and he would have still been visible to me, but he was gone. I have thought that it might have been interesting to have walked to the K-Mart parking lot to see if there was a vehicle with Oklahoma license plates. I've often wondered if he was an angel sent by God to test my generosity. If this was the case, then sadly I failed. I vow to not let this happen again. "Do not forget to entertain strangers for thereby some have entertained angels without knowing it" (Heb. 13:2).

Dean Lyon has his own business where he makes western-style lighting fixtures made from large, wooden, wagon wheels. One morning he had an unusual spiritual and ominous experience. This is how he reported it to me:

The Foreboding Stranger

It was in the spring of 1998 and I had been working seventy to eighty hours a week. My normal routine was to get up at 3:00 A.M., shower, and then go to the shop. And one morning, about 4:00 A.M. in the morning, I was at the shop drilling wagon wheels on the drill press. Whether it was the hair standing up on the back of my neck, or a cold breeze, I just felt a presence in the shop. The shop was very quiet, and as I turned around I saw a man dressed in black standing between the drill press and the work bench, six or seven feet away from me. He had on a black hat and either a black coat or black shirt and black pants. He didn't have a face (no facial features). His face was completely gray, and it appeared to be surrounded with a fine bright outline. I was visibly shaken and nervous, but I didn't feel threatened or fear. I'm not sure whether I blinked or turned around, but he was gone at that instance. I stood there for a minute, trying to figure out what had just taken place; what's happening here? I thought because of the many hours I had been working at the shop that maybe I was too tired. Anyway, I usually call my wife Emily at five o'clock to wake her up, but I immediately called her after I saw this person. She and I talked about this strange happening, which I knew was real. I believed that there must surely be some kind of sign or message which the person clothed in black was trying to convey to me, but I didn't know what it meant. But I knew it was real, it was absolutely real. Since then, Emily and I have shared this with some good friends of ours, and they've accepted my very unusual experience because I'm not a prevaricator.

It was in January, 1999 that I was diagnosed with prostate cancer. My thoughts immediately went back to the man dressed in black, who I had seen in my shop in the spring of 1998. It was then that I really discovered the message he was trying to convey to me.

As it turned out, I had prostate surgery, but the medical pathological report indicated that, even with the prostate removed, there still existed cancer cells at the margin; near where the prostate was.

As I reflect back, if I had heeded the warning from the man dressed in black, whether or not it was an angel, the message is very clear to me now that I was to take care of my health. And, instead of waiting, if I would have had my health checked when I first saw the man dressed in black, it's very likely the prostate cancer could have been completely eliminated.

Traci Lynn Rech was 12-years-old when her mother was diagnosed with cancer. Her mother died on Christmas Day 1994. Traci is now 18-years-old as she writes about her mother's battle with cancer and her angel experience. This is her story:

My Guardian Angel

All of the presents still sat under the tree in the corner of the living room. No one was really anxious to open any of them. Christmas was always a fun time at my house, but this year was very different. My mom loved Christmas. It was her favorite time of the whole year. She always said it doesn't matter what you get, but it is the thought that counts and being with the people that you love the most on this special day. She wanted my little brother and me to open the present that she got us. She wanted to make sure that we liked it because it was the last thing she would ever be able to give us. She sat in the chair and watched me open my present on the couch. As I opened it, I realized it was the Orlando Magic coat that I wanted. "Mom, thank you very much!" I said to her while I gave her a hug and kiss on the cheek. "Do you like it?" she said in a very soft voice. "Yes, mom, I love it." At the time I really did not care much about the coat. The only true Christmas present that everyone wanted was for my mom to get better and be happy like she was on every other Christmas.

This was the second time my mother had cancer. The first time she had ocular-melanoma, which is a very rare type of cancer of the eye. Since the cancer was affecting her eye sight she had to have her right eye removed. It was replaced with a glass one that looked just like the other one. It was very hard to tell which eye was real and which eye was fake. She would always flip it upside down when I walked into a room, because she knew I hated to look at it. It looked weird because one eye was looking at you while the other one was looking another direction.

A year later we found out that the cancer had spread to her liver. The doctors told her that she had an option to take chemotherapy or do nothing about the cancer. Chemotherapy is ". . . the treatment of disease-causing microorganism" (Thomas 335). My mom was a nurse and saw what chemotherapy did to some of her patients. She said she would never take chemotherapy because she did not want to spend the time she had left in pain and have her family watch her suffer. There was some hope that the cancer would shrink and then they would be able to remove it, but only if she took chemotherapy. My mother had my little brother and me still to raise, so she decided to take the chance on chemotherapy shrinking the cancer. She wanted to be able to watch her kids and grand kids grow up. She was only able to have three treatments.

There was no snow on the ground. This was very unusual for me, because Christmas always had been cold with lots of snow on the ground. It seemed like it was a spring day, instead it was Christmas. Everything was just fine, and I didn't think that my whole world would change over night, but how wrong I was. On Christmas Eve I knew that something was not right, when my mother asked, "Traci, will you hand me my purse?" "Why do you need it, mom?" "I have to get the number for Vase's [funeral home], so I can call them." I left it at that and did not say anything else, but I was only thirteen at the time so I did not think anything of it until the next day. Later on that day my grandma and grandpa arrived from Gillette [Wyoming] to spend Christmas with my mother. They had their whole car full of presents. It was really fun carrying all our presents inside our house. There were tons of presents under the tree. It was the most presents I had ever seen. I thought that it was going to be a fun Christmas.

That night we had to put my mom on oxygen because it was getting harder for her to breath on her own. She was not happy at all about that because she did not like the tubes up her nose. That night she was up all night in pain. There were many times that I heard her get up from sleeping in the chair to go to the bathroom. It was really hard for her to walk because the pain was so bad. She could not sleep in her bed anymore because it was hard to get in and out of it. The medicine was not helping her at all.

Christmas day we were all up really early with her. She sat in a living room chair with her eyes closed, while I sat next to her in a chair I'd taken from the kitchen. I held her hand as I played with her gold bracelet, spinning it around her wrist. She looked like a ghost, and her hands were ice cold, but she said that she was hot. She had sweat running down her forehead. I was crying, but I didn't want her to know that I was crying. She hated it when people cried around her, because I think she knew she was going to a better place.

There was a time that I had to leave because I could not take it any more. I knew that I was going to lose her. I did not want to lose her, but there was nothing I could do to stop it, except wish for a miracle to happen. I went and sat on the couch and curled up into a ball and cried even harder than before. I knew that she probably heard me, but I could not hold it in anymore. She did not have the energy to tell me to quit. I thought that she was just tired because she was up all night. It seemed her pain was getting worse hour by hour and that the morphine was not helping at all. I always thought she would be there to watch me grow up. One thing I really wanted was to have her watch me graduate from high school.

I was going to go to church and pray for her, but my dad said that I better stay home because I needed to be with my mom. While my mom was sitting in the chair holding my grandma's hand she looked up and said, "There are five angels standing in front of me." "Ruthie, it's okay to go. Go ahead and go with your daddy." My grandmother thought that one of the angels was my mom's dad. It was very quiet in the house because everyone was trying to listen to what my mom had to say because her voice was so soft. "There are seven angels in front of me now," my mother said. "Ruthie, we will understand if you go with the angels," grandma said.

My mom took a big breath, and we thought that she was gone, but she was still holding on. My sister brought over my nephews and nieces to say good-bye to her. It was my nephew Aaron's birthday, and my mom had always told him that he was very special to be born on the same day as Jesus. She gave my nephew, Kyle, and my niece,

Devan, a kiss good-bye and told them she loved them very much. She told Aaron happy birthday and that she loved him, and then she kissed him good-bye.

She took one more deep breath and her suffering and pain were gone. It was just like she went to sleep and never woke up. About an hour later, Vase's came and took her away on a gurney. She looked so much more peaceful than she did an hour before. I knew all of her pain was gone, but the pain of her leaving me was still there. I felt a part of me leave with her. As she laid there on the gurney, I held her hand and told her, "Mom, I love you very much and will always love you."

I realized then the real reason why she asked for Vase's number. She had planned all of her own funeral arrangements so that it was one less thing the family had to worry about. It was a blessing that we did not have to worry about what kind of funeral she would have liked. She knew she was going to die on the day she loved the most and was not scared at all because she was going to be with God. She just wanted the ones she loved most to be with her. She asked one thing of us and that was to be buried in her pajamas because that was the way she was most comfortable. She also told us that if we did not do that, she would come back and haunt us. We put her in angel pajamas with an angel blanket over her legs, because that was exactly what she was, an angel sent to us. The weird thing is there are many people that I have not seen in a long time and forgot what they looked like, but I can still remember the smile on my mother's face, the way she smiled, and especially the way she laughed. I am very happy that she is not in pain anymore, but there are also days I am angry at her for leaving me. I have to stop and think to myself that she is in a lot better place, a place where we would all like to be.

The rest of the day is just a blur because there were so many people that came and went. A lot of them were family. No one really cared about the presents under the tree. We opened all of my mom's presents. Most of them were angels just like her. We set them all around the house so that people who came over would remember her. This was really hard because she did not get to see any of them. I think of my mother and how she touched the lives of the people around her. To this day I get great compliments on how wonderful of a person my mother was. I am glad to see that her memory has lived on in so many people. That is one thing I hope to inherit from her.

Loss, a lot of people know what this word means, but do they know how it feels, that's the question. Christmas day was the day I learned what losing someone felt like and it will be one thing that I will never forget. I can remember it just like it was yesterday and I know it will be something I can never block out even if I wanted to. This was my mother's favorite day out of the whole year and I think that it was the best day for her to leave. She gave Christmas a new meaning to all of the people around her. I now know that she is in heaven, happy as can be, and watching over me as my guardian angel as I grow through life.

"MOM, I LOVE YOU!!!"

—Traci Lynn Rech

It was a couple of months after her mother's death that Traci received some reassurance from her mother.

This is how Traci described it:

Mom Is Watching Over Me

It was one evening in February, 1995 that my dad went out to have a social drink with a lady. I was home watching my little brother while dad was gone. I was only thirteen years old at the time, so I thought that it would be cool if I stayed up and talked on the phone to my friend, so that is what I did. While I was talking, I just happened to look down the hallway and there was my mother sitting in a chair with a white dress on, and her rings were sparkling in the dark. I was in shock, and I couldn't move from my bed. My mother then got up from the chair and moved to the window where she was looking out, and then she was gone. My friend that I was talking to on the phone thought that I was kidding around until he realized that I was scared to death. I called my older sister and told her what happened. I asked her if she knew how much longer before dad would be home, and she said, " Not much longer." After talking to my sister I hung up the phone and at that moment I heard the front door open. So I walked into the living room, and the first thing I said was, "Mom?" I then checked the door, and it was still locked so I looked out the window and saw that my dad's car was still gone. It was about five minutes later that my dad came home. I then realized that mom was here to watch over my little brother and me while dad was gone.

At times Traci has had dreams about her mother, and there was one particular time in which the dream was especially vivid and memorable. Traci told it this way:

A Vivid and Reassuring Dream

The time that I remember most was when I was at my mother's grave site with her best friend Bobbie. She was there too, not only to see my mother's grave site, but to visit her deceased husband's (Tom) grave site, which was located next to my mother's. Bobbie and I were talking about them when all of a sudden they both came out from behind a tree, and they asked what we were doing. They told us that they got a free day, and they got to came back to earth for this day. Bobbie and Tom went on their way, and my mom and I went back to our house. She helped me do things around the house. It was getting late and we were folding clothes, and my mom asked me to finish up folding the clothes while she took a shower. My mother showered and did her hair. She was putting on her guardian angel pins as she was walking out of her bedroom when she looked at me and said, "I don't have very many things to wear." She then gave me a big hug, kissed me, and told me she loved me and then she left. I looked out the window, and there above the porch window was an angel that made the whole sky shine brightly. It was the most beautiful thing I had ever seen. The angel took my mom's hand then they both disappeared into the air. I turned to my dad who was sitting on the couch playing Game Boy, and I told him that we should have kept all of my mom's clothes so that she would have something to wear when she came to visit. My dad and little brother, who was watching TV, looked at me like I was stupid before going back to what they were doing.

The reason I remember this dream so well is because she came here to see me and no one else.

Even though it was just a dream it seemed so real to me, and I believe that she was here with me at the time.

It is obvious in talking to Traci and from her writing that she and her mother were very close, and they loved each other immensely. Traci even wrote a poem for her mother which follows:

Who Is Going to Be There for Me?

There is not one day that goes by
that I don't think about you.
I shed a tear for you everyday.
I remember all the fun times
we had together.
Now that you are gone
I don't know what I am going to do.
Who is going to be there for me
when I am in trouble?
Who is going to be there for me
when I need a shoulder to cry on?
Who is going to be there for me
when I need someone to talk to?
You were there for me all my life.
Now that you are gone,
a part of me went with you.
Who is going to be there for me now?
Who?
Will you guide me through life,
make sure I learn from all of my mistakes
and make them right?
That is all I ask from you
now that you are gone.
P. S. I will always love you, MOM!

—Written By: Traci L. Rech
—Written For: Ruth E. Rech

Traci presents herself as a teenager who is mature beyond her young years, and I communicated this to her. She noted that others have told her the same thing. Traci, with the death of her mother, experienced a deep valley of life at a time when Traci, herself, was only thirteen years of age. She also shared other losses in her life and she, and her younger brother now live with their much older, married sister and her family. Traci has chosen to use her valleys of life as an opportunity to grow emotionally, mentally, and spiritually. She believes the emotional pain she has experienced has made her a stronger person and, no doubt she will draw upon this strength as she encounters other valleys which will come along in her life.

Marilyn Thomas has had her share of valleys in life. In one of her darkest valleys, she felt the hand of God and heard His voice. This is her story:

A Touch of Peace

A number of years ago, I was going through a divorce with three children under the age of ten. I had a good clerical job, but the cost of housing, feeding, clothing, and day care expenses caused me considerable stress.

In addition, I was commuting fifty miles each way to my job. I struggled with the knowledge that if an emergency arose with one of the children, it would take me at least an hour to get to them.

I had no family to help out. Friends were always ready to oblige a request for help, but I didn't want to turn into a "taker."

Both of my sons had been diagnosed with ADHD (Attention Deficit/Hyperactivity Disorder), which added to the pressure I felt. Even with them on medication, a good day for me was when the school did not call me regarding my sons' behavior. Scheduling their medical appointments was like walking a tight rope. My first responsibility was to my children, but I needed my job. I had to take an entire afternoon off to accomplish a one hour checkup for them.

My employer was patient at first, but I knew each time I requested time off for the boys' appointments, it grew thinner. The pressures were mounting. I felt as though I could snap at any moment.

I became tense and irritable from all the demands. With no family in the area and the father living out of state, I felt so alone.

One day a certified letter came from the IRS. It stated my wages were going to be garnished for taxes owed on a joint tax return from several years back.

I wasn't concerned at first because that issue had been taken care of in the divorce decree. The children's father took full responsibility for payment of the debt.

Upon calling the IRS, I was told that no payments had been made on the liability and that the divorce decree was a civil matter, not federal. I would have to pay the sum of $4,000, then collect it from my ex-husband.

I hung up the phone and sat stunned, letting it slowly sink in. The evening passed as usual on the outside, but inside my nerves were raw. I couldn't take it any more. I put the children to bed then slipped into the shower and began to cry, softly at first, then the sobs began, being ever so careful not to let the children hear me. I prayed that the water would wash all my problems away, but it didn't.

After the shower, I crawled into bed. I was lying on my side in my dark bedroom, still sobbing and asking God for help; any help. I desperately wanted any shred of strength to come to my aid.

It was as this point that I felt a very slight, gentle pressure on my lean shoulder. It felt like a very warm hand. I looked up, but saw nothing. The touch was so gentle, yet so powerful. In that instant I felt the most overwhelming sense of peace. I heard the words, "You are not alone. I am with you."

Was it the hand of God? I'm certain it was. I have never felt such peace, such a lightening of mortal trials, such a sense of goodness and strength. I knew I was not alone in that room anymore, nor was I alone any longer to face the years ahead. He came to me when I needed Him most, and His hand has not failed me since.

My oldest son is now twenty-one. I think back to that "touch of peace" and the many times I called upon it through the years.

Be open to Him. He will be there for you too!

Marilyn had another spiritual experience. In her own words:

A Guiding Light

My three children and I had fallen asleep in front of the TV one night. I woke up in the night, looked at them all snug in their sleeping bags, then went on to my bedroom, and slipped back into a nice restful sleep.

A sound in the pitch darkness came first. What was it? A muffled cry? Where was it coming from? It drew closer, but not louder. It was stifled somehow.

Then I felt movement on my mattress accompanied by the muffled cry. I reached out. It was my 8-year-old son. Something was terribly wrong! I could hear him, but couldn't see him. I could feel his arms slashing at the darkness. I could hear his muffled cries for help. I needed to see what was wrong.

At that moment a bright, but hazy white light encircled his small body. He was choking. I was not yet aware of the light around him, only the need to get help quickly. I grabbed for the phone on my nightstand and dialed 911. The reality of the light struck me at the moment the dispatcher asked questions and gave commands. I wouldn't have been able to see to dial the phone for help without the ready availability of the light. I would not have been able to quickly help my son without "the light".

The police arrived very quickly and took over my gasping son, while I awaited the ambulance. They arrived quickly also and whisked him off to the hospital.

He had fallen asleep with a piece of bubble gum in his mouth. It had slipped down his throat and was teetering at the top of his esophagus, obstructing most of his airways.

Even in the midst of panic and confusion I wondered at "the light". Was it his Guardian Angel? Was it the omnipotent Light of God? Was it both?

Ten years later, I still remember the light as if it was yesterday.

A light to guide us through a storm. A great light of Heaven surely did shine for us that night.

My cousin Dixie, who has a twin, Donna, was involved in a tragic, car accident shortly after I had been on leave from the Marine Corps. Dixie has always seemed to have a spiritual intuitiveness about her. This is Dixie's story:

A Prayer Answered

It was a chilly November (1957) evening when my dear friend and I experienced her death in a car accident. As we were traveling on a country road we were approaching a "T" intersection, which was not indicated by a road sign. We stopped abruptly as the car smashed into the dirt embankment. Sue was killed instantly, and I was tossed under the dash, my legs denting it in and my head hit the dash and broke the windshield. When the noise settled down I was better able to assess my injuries. It was noticeable that my friend, Sue, was gone. I prayed for God to forgive her of any sins and that she would rest in heaven. I felt His presence, and I also prayed to live. That is obvious as I am here writing my memory of that long ordeal.

I was in the hospital in critical condition with a tube down my throat, a cast on one leg, the other leg in traction, a head concussion, and ruptured vocal cords. I drifted in and out of consciousness. During one my "outs," I had what I thought was a dream. My dear friend, and someone with her, were chasing me around a cemetery. It lasted only seconds. Then during another "out," I dreamed I was kneeling down at a tree stump, and I looked up and a gate opened. Sue and another person, a tall boy who looked like her, floated out of the gate. We exchanged glances and they floated back and the gate closed. It was a beautiful garden scene to which they returned. I believe it was about then that I opened my eyes to reality. My mother and aunt were standing by my bed. They had just been to Sue's funeral and they spoke of the beautiful service for her. They noted that Sue had gone to heaven to be with her brother who died when he was a baby many years ago. It made sense to me now that the tall boy I saw in my dream was Sue's brother, who in heaven, had continued to grow. I did not know that Sue had a brother who died when he was a baby. I now questioned whether it had been a dream that I saw him in or whether it was spiritual vision. I concluded that it was God's way of telling me that, yes indeed, He had answered my prayer, and Sue was in heaven.

Months later, when I was able to get around, Sue's parents took me to the cemetery where she was buried. It was the same cemetery in my dream. The cemetery was in another town and not previously known to me.

It was a long time before I ever discussed this as people are often skeptical when they hear experiences like this. Being sedated a lot in the hospital, I may, at times, have been hallucinating, but I know what I saw and felt. There was no greater peace than what I felt!

I have wanted to write about this for years and I feel that this was a perfect opportunity to share my experience. I have had many prayers answered and I feel the enrichment of believing in every day life.

Thank you dear cousin Paul for providing me the opportunity to share my special spiritual experience with you.

I have never meet Ann Lynn Graham in person, but we have communicated a few times by phone, e-mail, and letter. An angel story about a hitchhiker in California led me to locating her. She is still in the process of trying to assist me in acquiring that story for my book. My impression about Ann is that she is moving along nicely on the spiritual path. She has her own special spiritual experience to tell about her daughter Evangel and her three children as they came out of a large shopping mall in Sioux Falls, S.D. This is how Ann told it.

Protected by the Hand of God

In 1996, a little over three years ago, I was meeting regularly with some women for a Bible study. One day we were talking about how the evil one is out to destroy, and often gets at us through our families. So, it was with delight that we shared with one another how wonderful it was to have that hedge of protection from God around us all. Not only are we promised that, "The eyes of the Lord are on those who fear him" (Ps. 33), but that, "The angel of the Lord encamps around those who fear him, and he delivers them." (Ps. 34) Rejoicing in words like these, we prayed for our families, our children, and grandchildren.

The day after our study and prayer time, I received a phone call from our daughter Evangel. She and her dentist husband Scott and their four children live about fifty miles from us in Brandon, South Dakota. With tears noticeable in her voice, she related to me an experience she had had with her children just the day before when they had been to nearby Sioux Falls.

She had dropped 11-year-old Whitney off at lessons and went with her three youngest children

(Bryan, Kelley, and Lyndsey) to a catalog department in a store in the large Sioux Falls mall.

When the four of them came out of the store, Evangel noticed a van parked at the curb in front of them, waiting to load a TV. Their red suburban was parked just yards away, but they had to cross a street, which ran through the mall parking lot in order to reach it. She warned the children, as she always does, "Watch out for cars." Looking herself in both directions, and seeing it was safe, she added, "No cars." As they walked behind the van, Bryan (who just turned nine) and Kelley (nearly six years old) trotted ahead, deciding to see which one of them could reach their suburban first. However, just as they started to run, they literally and simultaneously bounced backwards two steps and both of them exclaimed, "WHOA!"

At the same moment, Evangel and Lyndsey (three and a half) were also stopped, though not as dramatically. Evangel recalls that she didn't know why they stopped, nor why they both made one step backwards. But is was only then, after all four of them had been stopped from emerging from behind the parked van and they were all in a safe place, that they caught the first glimpse of danger. At that instant a car whizzed by within eighteen inches of Bryan and Kelly.

Evangel knew immediately in her heart that God had sent angels to stop them, and He had done so before any of them had sensed any danger. Had the Lord not stopped them and kept them in the safe place behind the van, they would have been in the path of that car that none of them had seen until it whizzed by.

Knowing how close they had come to tragedy, Evangel was shaken and immediately felt weak. At the same time, she was touched with amazement as she recalled seeing Bryan and Kelley bounce backwards, as if they had both, at the same instant, run into an invisible rubber wall. Evangel and Lyndsey stepped backwards too, without knowing why or even thinking about it. None of them, but God, had seen that car.

The children, too, were amazed. Bryan told the experience in the days following to anyone who would listen. He told of how he had been stopped in his tracks and had bounced backward, yet hadn't seen anything or didn't know what caused him and his sister to bounce like they did at the same time. Kelley still recalls that whatever it was they ran into, "It was soft." And she still laughs when she remembers how surprised she was and the reaction she and Bryan both had. They each said, "Whoa!" (like WOW!) before they even saw what danger they were in.

That night, Evangel had a hard time keeping the tears back as she thought of how she could have been planning her children's funerals were it not for the Lord's marvelous protection that day. She knew in her heart, that though none of them saw God's angels with their eyes, there were angels there, which God had used to keep them from harm. God had intervened even before they knew they were in danger. She cried herself to sleep that night as she thanked God for sparing her family.

Even now, when we talk with the children or one another, we are awe struck with the Lord's grace and loving care for us. He really is an awesome God! And this is certainly one family to whom those verses in Psalm 91 are very real: "He will give His angels charge over you, to keep you in all your ways. They will lift you up in their hands, lest you dash your foot against a stone."

Kim Johnson is a niece of twins Dixie and Donna mentioned earlier and the daughter of Delbert and Mary Ann Crawford. Delbert is a brother to Dixie and Donna. Kim is a special education teacher in Iowa. Kim and her family experienced a great loss in their family, but God provided them with loving reassurance that things were going to be all right. This is how Kim shared the experience.

Daddy in the Clouds and Orange Butterflies Galore

On 1 August 1999 my husband was killed in a water skiing accident on the Mississippi River. He was 31-years-old and the father of two little girls (Lindsey, age 4 and Taylor, age 6). He was buried on Wednesday in a traditional Catholic service.

The girls were both involved in planning some of the service and picking out the place where Mark would be buried. Prior to Mark's death we had attended church fairly regularly and believed that our girl's and ourselves had a good faith in God.

The Tuesday before the funeral, our girls attended a grief class sponsored by the funeral home. During the class, the lady talking to Taylor and Lindsey used the parallel of a caterpillar and a butterfly with dying and receiving a new and better body in Heaven. The kids seemed to understand this, and we continued to talk about Heaven at home. We read in the book of Revelations about the streets of gold and the description of

Heaven. Through all of this I was proud of the children's faith and their desire to understand.

The first "little miracle" happened for Taylor on Wednesday afternoon, the day of the funeral. She and her cousin Kayla were in the back yard lying on the trampoline and looking up into the clouds. She told Kayla she saw her daddy. After a few days and some encouragement by her aunt, she told me of the experience. She said, "I could see daddy. He didn't have any legs, but he was smiling, and he had one eye closed." I asked her if she meant that he was winking and she said, "Yes." She continued to explain, "There were angels around him. They had wings, but I didn't know any of them." Taylor tends to be a worrier and I truly believe that the angels brought Mark to her to show her that her daddy was all right. A few nights later Taylor said the most profound thing to me. She said, "The earth is really like a hotel. It is not our real home; we are just visiting. Heaven is our real home." She explained it perfectly. The faith of a child is simple and pure.

The second miracle happened for all of us about one month after Mark died. It was a Wednesday afternoon at about five o'clock. It had been a long and exhausting day for me emotionally. I had been to the business that sells headstones, trying to select a headstone for Mark's grave. I had finally sat down on our deck in the back yard and was reading a book on grief. I really lost it and began to cry and sob. I looked up and saw an orange butterfly and remembered how it had become a sign for us. While visiting Mark's grave site, we had experienced butterflies while sitting on his grave. It, however, was not bringing me much comfort on this day. I can remember thinking that I didn't want a butterfly, I wanted Mark! As I looked around I saw the most amazing thing. There were orange butterflies flying all over our back yard and in among the trees of our neighbors' and good friend's yard. It was impossible to count, but there must have been at least fifty of them. We called our neighbors, and they came over. They commented on how many there were and how high these butterflies were flying. Butterflies usually fly low, but these were flying as high as birds. The butterflies stayed in the same area and did not cross over into the yards to the right or left of our property. After twenty to thirty minutes the butterflies slowly dispersed.

At the funeral home we were offered the opportunity to buy thumb print necklaces of Mark's thumb print. I bought one for myself and one for Taylor and Lindsey. I explained to the girls that we would only wear these necklaces on special days as they were expensive and the girls were a little young to be responsible for them. I did, however, tell them it was a sign that Mark is okay, that God is with our family, and He'll help us. They could wear them on November 3rd, Mark's birthday. The day before his birthday, I searched frantically around the house for the necklaces. I found Lindsey's in the bathroom closet. Why, I don't know. Grieving people sometimes do weird things. I could not find Taylor's. I decided it would show up, and I let her wear mine on his birthday. About a week later, we went out for dinner and when we came home the house was dark. As I went upstairs to put my pajamas on there was a flashlight on in my bedroom. I went over to pick it up, and amazingly it was pointing directly to Taylor's thumb print necklace. It lay on the floor by my bed in plain sight.

Other things have happened to us, and I really do believe they are angel experiences. Taylor had a loose tooth one night and asked me to pull it right before bed. Mark had always pulled the teeth at our house, as I am rather squeamish. As I tried to pull it, I discovered it just wasn't ready and was still attached rather tightly in one corner. I said we'd try again the next day. However, I didn't get that opportunity because when Taylor woke up the next morning her tooth was missing. She found it under her pillow with not a sign of blood or redness. She said to me, "Maybe it was daddy."

In his tiny book, *Angels, God's Secret Agents,* Billy Graham, states this about angels…" They are God's messengers whose chief business is to carry out His orders in the world. He has given them an ambassadorial charge. He has designated and empowered them as holy deputies to perform works of righteousness (pg., 14).

The most important characteristic of angels is not that they have power to exercise control over our lives, but that they work on our behalf" (Billy Graham, *Angels, God's Secret Agents,* Nashville, TN: Word Publishing, 1994, pg. 49).

Angel stories can be very interesting and reassuring. There is a sense of wonder in hearing stories about them and no doubt a sense of awe to those who have had angel encounters. I understand we are not to praise angels, but to praise God who created them and has assigned them to work on our behalf. It's reassuring to know they are in our midst, and with the increase in angel books and stories in the last decade, it makes one wonder if something spiritual is forthcoming.

I hope you enjoyed your journey through this angel chapter.

VI

The Greatest Gift, and It's Free!

"Store up riches for yourselves in heaven, where moths and rust cannot destroy, and robbers cannot break in and steal. For your heart will always be where your riches are."

—Matthew 6:20-21

The day after Thanksgiving in America hordes of people rush out for a buying spree. They scurry about through the cold and snow, going from store to store in an effort to buy, buy, buy. The stores, decorated to entice us into the Christmas spirit, are filled with plentiful gift ideas for all members of the family. Christmas songs continually fill the air in stores throughout the holiday shopping season, hoping to elevate our mood and facilitate our weakness for spending during this festive time of the year. There is hardly a retail store which does not participate in seducing us into spending our money.

Families decorate their Christmas tree, their house, trees on their lawn, etc. Special recognition is given to houses which have the fanciest or most decorations. Towns and cities decorate their streets, trees, buildings, etc. with many colorful sparkling lights which easily catch our eye. Businesses and Wall Street investors hope we spend money enthusiastically so their profits will be robust.

On Christmas morning, large and small beautifully wrapped presents abound under the tree. Family members are excited as they quickly and enthusiastically tear open their numerous gifts, leaving them with a feeling of joy for all they have received.

However, for some children, such as a child in the inner city or in Appalachia, they are fortunate to receive even one gift for Christmas, and if they do, I imagine they cherish it immensely. For these families, their money runs out before the end of the month. They often lack money for which to buy sufficient food, heat, clothing, and medicine. At the end of the month these families are eating a diet consisting mainly of starches, and they lack laundry money to wash their clothes. It is a never ending struggle for the parent(s) to financially provide for their impoverished family. The loss of hope and emotional depression are always nearby, hovering as a vulture waiting, waiting for the parent(s) to give up the struggle for survival. But, for these families, as for everyone and all families, there is the grandest of all gifts that awaits their discovery!

In the "Charlie Brown Christmas" movie, Charlie Brown is humiliated by Lucy as she severely berates him for getting, what she perceives as, a terribly scraggly Christmas tree for them to decorate. Shortly, Linus is standing in the center of a stage, and with Charlie Brown looking on, Linus tells the Bible story of the birth of Christ. "And there were in the same country shepherds abiding in the field, keeping watch over their flock by night. And, lo, the angel of the Lord came upon them, and the glory of the Lord shone round about them; and they were sore afraid. And the angel said unto them, "Fear not, for behold, I bring you good tidings of great joy, which shall be to all people. For unto you is born this night in the city of David, a Savior, which is Christ the Lord. And this shall be a sign unto you; you shall find the babe wrapped in swaddling clothes, lying in a manger. And suddenly there was with the angel a multitude of the heavenly host praising God and saying, Glory to God in the highest, and on earth peace, good will toward men" (Luke 2:8-14 KUV). And that is what Christmas is all about Charlie Brown."

What would you desire if you could ask for any gift, with no consideration of the cost? For many, millions of dollars might come to mind or to be a perfect physical specimen, to have the perfect spouse, to have perfect children, or the perfect job.

I wonder how much thought any of us really gives as to why we celebrate Christmas, the day Christ was born. It seems, at times, commercialism and too much spending on earthly gifts has squeezed Christ to a secondary role. Various church denominations do their part in trying to keep the day of Christ's birth alive.

It is a very moving experience to attend the Christmas Eve services in a Methodist church and in many other church denominations, too. The church, filled with parishioners, sing their last hymn, "Silent Night, Holy Night," with the electrical lights off and each person holding a tiny lit candle. It's wonderful and the meaning of why we celebrate Christmas greatly touches our heart and soul as we sing joyfully!

God has given us the gift of Jesus, but it is what Jesus did that is the greatest gift we can receive, the gift of eternal life. There is no gift which can compare! On *Earth*, we seem to be mainly concerned with material possessions, drinking alcohol, power, sex, violence, getting high on illegal drugs, and other behaviors which are detrimental to the human race with little or no pursuit of spiritual matters. "Set your minds on things that are above, not on things that are on earth" (Col. 3:2, RSV).

Jesus was crucified on the cross, buried in a tomb, and rose from the dead on the third day, the day we celebrate Easter. If we believe this and declare Jesus to be our Lord and Savior, then we, by God's grace, will receive the grandest gift of all, eternal life with our Lord in Heaven! Praise God for His grand gift to us! We just have to do our part in receiving this free gift. What a shame it would be for anyone not to receive it, being available to rich and poor, all races, all ages, everyone who hears the Good News. Our Lord loves us with unimaginable, unconditional love, and He wants us to have this most precious free gift.

> Jesus said, "I am the resurrection and the life. Whoever believes in me will live, even though he dies; and whoever lives and believes in me will never die." (John 11:25-26, TEV)

> For by grace you have been saved through faith, and this is not your own doing, it is the gift of God—not because of works, lest any man should boast. (Eph. 2:8-9, RSV)

God *is* love. He loves us with pure, unconditional love. He loves us regardless of how much we mess up our lives. He never gives up on us, never. He is forever patiently waiting for us to come to Him. Unfortunately, it's often when we are experiencing great emotional pain and want relief, that we desire to turn to His gentle, waiting, loving arms. He loves us so much that He allowed His Son, Jesus, to die on the cross with His blood, wiping away our sins and purchasing our opportunity for the grand gift of eternal life in heaven. One of my favorite Bible passages regarding God's love is: ". . . God is love, and anyone who lives in love is living in God and God is living in him [her]" (1 John 4:16).

If we stay in the love mode, we can be sure God is dwelling in us, and we are dwelling in Him. The farther we are from the love mode (loving attitude), the farther we are from God.

I, in no way want you, the reader, to think that I am "holier than thou" because I am not. Too many times in my sixty plus years of life I have not been in the love mode, and it is still a challenge for me. Even though I have had very meaningful prayer experiences and have felt inspired by God as I write this book, I am but a spiritual infant. In all of my years, I have taken but a few steps on the spiritual path, which is infinite. Nonetheless, God still provides me with His great gift. Praise be to God!

Jesus gave us examples in the Bible, trying to get us to understand how precious this gift (eternal life) is, which He later purchased for us with His blood and death:

> Again, the Kingdom of Heaven is like a pearl merchant on the look out for choice pearls. He discovered a real bargain—a pearl of great value— and sold everything he owned to purchase it! (Matt. 13:45)

> The Kingdom of Heaven is like a treasure a man discovered in a field. In his excitement he sold everything he owned to get enough money to buy the field—and get the treasure, too! (Matt. 13:44)

I strongly believe if we *choose* to be saved into eternal life, when we get to Heaven, a loving God will certainly provide us with the opportunity to continue to grow in spiritual knowledge and strength. Also, I believe that our spiritual growth here on earth will determine, if we are saved, our placement level in heaven. If we are saved into eternal life, but have grown little spiritually on earth, then I believe we can expect to be placed at a lower spiritual level in heaven. Jesus said, "There are many rooms in my Father's house and I am going to prepare a place for you. I would not tell you this if it were not so" (John 14:2-3, TEV).

I recall reading about Dr. Norman Vincent Peale, the great minister of Marble Collegiate Church (founded in 1628) in New York City. When he died, a relative, I believe, wrote about how she saw a huge choir singing praises to God for Dr. Peale. I would expect people who have attained great spiritual growth and/or spiritual accomplishments here on earth to be placed at a much higher level in heaven than those of us who have grown or accomplished less spiritually.

"For God so loved the world that he gave his only Son, so that whoever believes in him may not perish, but may have eternal life. Indeed, God sent the Son into the world, not to condemn the world, but that the world might be saved through him" (John 3:16-17, RSV). I would urge you, today, to choose to take the necessary steps so you will receive the Greatest Gift of All, *ETER-NAL LIFE!*

> Thanks be to God for his indescribable gift. (2 Cor. 9:15, NIV)

> Thank God for his Son—his Gift too wonderful for words. (2 Cor. 9:15)

> God has reserved for his children the priceless gift of eternal life. It is kept in Heaven for you. It is pure and spotless. It is beyond the reach of change and decay. (1 Pet. 1:4)

VII

Be a Channel

*"Let your light shine before people, so that
they will see the good things you do and praise your
Father in heaven."*

—Matthew 5:16

It was a few years after our divorce, and before I
moved to Bethel, Alaska, to work, that another thought
came to me which I felt was God inspired. I believe this
because of its clarity and how it has remained with me
over these many years. I have felt that it was the Holy
Spirit who planted the thought in my head.

I was standing in the living room of my comfortable
mobile home in Iowa City, and I can even remember I
was facing north, when the following thought was in my
head: *"Be a channel through which God can touch others in a
positive and spiritual way."* I pretty much forgot about it,
went to Alaska, and continued on my way until the cancer struck, then this thought strongly impressed itself on
my mind again.

I now feel a greater need to be receptive to God, so
He can use me as a channel through which He can touch
others in a positive and spiritual way. When I sense that
I may be in a situation where God may desire to use me
as a channel through which He can do His great work, I
usually pray for God's guidance and for the correct choice

121

of words and actions to use that will satisfy His will. When I have the thought or feeling that I need to do something for someone to lift their spirits, I usually give them a copy of *Where Angels Walk,* but it partially depends upon the situation. If I give them a book I usually say a prayer that God will touch them spiritually, mentally, and emotionally as they read the book chosen for them.

I believe that not only does God have a plan for each one of us, but that God works through people to accomplish things. We can all be channels through which God can touch the lives of those around us in a positive and spiritual way. Jesus said, "The words I say are not my own, but are from my Father who lives in me. And he does his work through me" (John 14:10). The apostle Paul, who wrote numerous books of the Bible (New Testament), was a messenger, or channel, through which he brought the message of Jesus to the gentiles. Paul said, "We are Christ's ambassadors. God is using us to speak to you" (2 Cor. 5:20). "This is Paul writing to you, chosen by God to be Jesus Christ's messenger" (Eph. 1:1). Just as God did his work through Jesus and the apostle Paul, God can do his work through us if we are willing to be a channel for Him.

I feel that this may be part of God's plan for me, but this is still unclear. I know it is delightful to perceive myself as a channel for God, and it is enjoyable to be a part in touching someone's life in a positive and spiritual way. I believe God especially finds favor when we act as a channel and do positive and spiritual things anonymously. This has its own special joy! *"He who refreshes others will himself be refreshed"* (Prov. 11:25, NIV).

"It is God himself who has made us what we are and given us new lives through Christ Jesus; and long ages ago he planned that we would spend these lives in helping others" (Eph. 2:10). I believe part of God's purpose for each one of us is that we are here on this earth to help others, to be a channel through which God can do His work.

On the Daytime Emmy Awards 15 May 1998, Oprah Winfrey won the Emmy for the best daytime talk show host. In her eloquent acceptance speech, Oprah said, "Ever since I was a little girl, my prayer to God has been, use me, use me." God has used her talents to touch many lives in a positive, and I believe, spiritual way. She has been a channel through which God has touched millions of lives.

We need to put our faith in God and have our will become His will, becoming dependent upon Him for all our needs. This will allow God to use our talents more effectively in touching the hearts and souls of those with whom we come in contact.

"It is God who does the work in us, and it makes sense that the more we trust in Him and the less we depend on ourselves, the more He is able to do" (*Power In Praise*, pg. 48).

*   *   *   *   *

During January of 1990, as I was still working for the Lower Kuskokwim School District in Bethel, Alaska, I made arrangements with Himalayan Travel in Connecticut to travel (hike) to Machu Picchu in Peru in July.

In February or March of that same year I received a very small newspaper clipping from a first cousin. It told of a French couple who were traveling in Peru and were taken off a bus and killed. The article also stated that the United States State Department urged Americans not to travel to Peru because of the danger of the Shining Path terrorist group having armed conflict with the Peruvian Government. It certainly caught my attention, but my love of hiking in nature, my enthusiasm for adventure, and my great interest in seeing the Inca Indian ruins at Machu Picchu (one of the great wonders of the world), as well as experiencing Peru and its culture, kept my focus on completing the trip.

In July, after visiting Mark and his family in Kansas, Mark drove me to the Kansas City International Airport for my flight to the Miami Airport, completing the first leg of my trip to Lima, Peru. I arrived at the Miami Airport about 10:00 P.M., and my flight to Lima was not until 1:00 A.M. I sat down in a waiting area near the Peruvian Airline check-in area for a long wait. Shortly, a woman, I'll call her Michelle, initiated conversation with me. Michelle was a special education teacher in Boston. She had a home in Lima, and she was returning there for the summer. She showed me a *Soldier of Fortune* magazine. It had an article in it about the Shining Path Rebels and their activities. Michelle said she had friends in Boston who wanted to visit her in Peru this summer, but she advised them against this because of the danger to tourists.

I was made aware that many of the people in Peru were very poor, particularly the Indians, who are descendants of the Incas. Due to their severe poverty, she informed me, there are lots of thieves and pickpockets. I've heard stories where people sometimes are so desperate for goods in which to use or sell, that tourists with backpacks in crowds have had their packs cut at the bottom and some of the contents stolen. I thought of my soft sided unlocked stuffed luggage and Northface backpack, both out of my sight as they were transported from airline to airline to be picked up by me in Lima. Would they be there in Lima intact or would they have been ransacked along the way? Knowing they would be sitting somewhere in the Peruvian Airline's baggage area for three hours before the plane took off made me uneasy. I began wondering, what am I getting myself into?

Shortly after midnight we began checking in with the airline, getting our seat assignment, etc. Michelle asked the airline representative if she could be assigned a seat next to me. I assisted her with her carry on items as we boarded the plane a little before 1:00 A.M. We talked and dozed until we arrived at the Lima Airport at 7:00 A.M. My passport was quickly checked as Michelle and I went through this checkpoint. We retrieved our luggage from the baggage area, and thankfully, my luggage and backpack were still intact.

Himalayan Travel was supposed to have a representative at the airport to meet me. Standing with my back to a wall, I vigilantly guarded Michelle's and my luggage while she wandered about in the small airport lobby looking for someone holding up a Himalayan Travel sign in English, which was to guide me in locating them. I saw two or three people holding up travel agency signs, but none from Himalayan. After a while Michelle came back with a man she knew. She said this man, now a taxi driver, used to have some connections with Himalayan Travel. She had talked him into dropping her off at her destination and me off at my downtown Lima Hotel. She spoke to him in Spanish, so I didn't know what they were saying. On our way to his cab, she told me not to pay him when I got to my hotel because he could get reimbursed by Himalayan Travel.

Later, at a very old, historic hotel in the city center of Lima, a representative from Himalayan Travel contacted me. He informed me that they were expecting me that evening, not early morning, which was the reason they were not at the airport to meet me. I have often wondered what I would have done had Michelle not initiated conversation with me in the Miami Airport. I might have waited 10-12 hours before a Himalayan Travel representative would have shown up. Being unable to communicate in Spanish, who knows what would have taken place.

I don't believe Michelle was an angel sent by God to assist me in my plight, but I firmly believe God used her as a channel through which He could help me avoid the uncomfortable situation in which I would have found myself. The outcome could not have run more smoothly. And this is just one of the many ways which God helps us in our time of need. He knows what is going to take place, and He is often working a head of time to lay the ground work for a safe outcome for us. If we are not on the spiritual path, we may attribute these good outcomes to luck or our own wit. If God or His angels are involved, we can be assured of the outcome.

*   *   *   *   *

In August 1996, the day before students were to return to their classrooms for the beginning of the 1996-1997 school year, all support staff met in a high school auditorium for introductions of new staff. Changes that would be implemented for the upcoming school year were also presented and discussed. School support staff consisted of numerous special education teachers, counselors, nurses, speech and language therapists, social workers, occupational therapists, physical therapists, and school psychologists. At the close of the meeting I was about to exit the door when a special education support staff member approached me. I knew of her, but I had never worked with her in any of the many, district, school buildings. She informed me that she had been recently diagnosed with breast cancer and that she wanted to talk with me. I strongly suspect that someone told her to talk with me, possibly because of what I had gone through with my cancer.

It was a couple of weeks later when she (I'll call her Susan) came to my office at Yellowstone Elementary. I had prepared myself for her visit by gathering numerous

Author at Machu Picchu—Inca Indian Ruins (Peru)

books, which I thought might bring comfort to her, one of which was Merlin Carothers' *Power In Praise*.

We talked about Susan's difficult health problem and the treatment she was to go through. I shared about my cancer and my experience of going through all of those chemotherapy sessions: the needles, methotrexate, nitrogen mustard, and VP-16. I expressed my disappointment of the return of my cancer, but that it is okay, that God has a plan for me, as He does for everyone, and that I just need to trust that He is going to work it out for me. I shared in detail some of my own prayer experiences with Susan, including the time when I felt particularly close to God and the time when I was struggling emotionally and had lost all hope. I told her of the delightful angel stories experienced by Bert, Brenda, and Vivian (Trudi's mother). I reassured her that we are in for quite a grand, spiritual experience when we die if we are spiritually prepared, believed that Jesus died for our sins, and we trusted Him to be our Lord and Savior. I expressed that we are very fortunate to have the opportunity to receive the precious gift of eternal life.

There came a point during my sharing of many things with Susan that she unexpectedly said, "I am feeling a sense of peace, and I wish my husband could talk with you." After about two and a half hours Susan left with the many books I had loaned and given to her. Shortly after she left I felt a sense of joy and the following thought was in my head, "Paul, you need to write a book." This book would encompass some of the same material that I had shared with Susan and more. It would be written specifically for those people, who themselves or a loved one, are facing a life threatening health problem, someone with cancer, a failing heart, kidney failure, serious diabetes, pneumonia, etc.; and it would hopefully provide the reader with a sense of great peace and reassurance. A message that would allow the reader to be able to say, "I have serious cancer, but it's okay because Jesus is my salvation, and God has given me the great gift of eternal life. My spirit will live forever in peace and love beyond my comprehension!" or "My heart is not able to do it's job effectively and I don't like it, but it's all right because I'm spiritually saved; and God has a grand plan for me! Thank you God for your grand gift to me of eternal life! Praise be to God!"

As I began writing this book I realized that I had been a channel, a channel through which God had the opportunity to communicate to Susan through me. I trust that the words I expressed were God inspired and were what He wanted her to hear.

Joy comes to us when we desire to be a channel through which God can touch the many lives of those in which we come in contact, however brief. Love, joy, peace, and a feeling of being close to God envelope us at that moment we realize we have been a spiritual channel for God to communicate to another individual. Our prayer to God needs to be, "God, help me to be receptive to your guidance and get myself out of the way so you can communicate your message to the person for whom you want me to be a channel." The credit goes to God, not us. We provide the means and God provides the message.

If you or a loved one are facing a challenging health situation, I pray that after reading the words in this book, that God will permeate your being with love, joy, peace, and comfort, that you will feel that things will be all right regardless of the outcome. I wrote this book with the sole purpose of reassuring all of those who are staring death in the face, those whose health situation fills them with great uncertainty, those who feel great loneliness, those who feel scared, and those whose life situation has caused them to have lost all hope.

The 23rd Psalm (KJV) does not say, "Yea, though I walk *into* the valley of the shadow of death . . . ," but rather:

> . . . Yea, though I walk *through* the
> valley of the shadow of death, I will
> fear no evil: for thou art with me;
> thy rod and thy staff they comfort me.
> Thou preparest a table before
> me in the presence of mine enemies:
> thou anointest my head with oil;
> my cup runneth over.
> Surely goodness and mercy shall
> follow me all the days of my life:
> and I will dwell in the house of the
> LORD forever.

We need to realize at any age, but especially if we're facing a life threatening situation, that we are spiritual beings. "We are spiritual beings having a human experience" (Teilhard de Chardin, French philosopher). Our body is the house for our spirit and soul for as long as we're physically alive. We're all on a spiritual journey and when we die, our spirit will leave our ravaged body.

I had an aunt, now deceased, who used to operate the Crawford Nursing Home in the 1950s in my high school town of Fairfield. Her name was Elsa, but we called her Elsie. She was the mother of Delbert and twins Dixie and Donna mentioned in the angel chapter. She was also the mother of Dale and Dean, both deceased. Elsie was a licensed practical nurse, and she loved taking care of elderly people. Daily she dispensed medication to all within her care. One day she gave medication to an elderly lady. Immediately after the lady consumed the medicine she died, and Elsie saw the lady's spirit come out of her chest area and ascend. Yes, we are spiritual beings!

... Our earthly bodies which die and decay are
different from the bodies we shall have when we
come back to life again, for they will never die.
(1 Cor. 15:42)

... But all who become Christ's will have the
same kind of body as his—a body from heaven.
(1 Cor. 15:48)

For our earthly bodies, the ones we have now
that can die, must be transformed into heavenly
bodies that cannot perish but will live forever. (1
Cor. 15:53)

God allowed his son Jesus to die the terrible death
on the cross to pay for our sins and on the third day he
rose from the dead, and if we believe this and declare
Him to be our Lord and Savior, then by God's grace, we
are assured of life eternal.

"God so loved the world that he gave his only Son,
so that everyone who believes in him may not perish, but
may have eternal life. Indeed, God did not send the Son
into the world to condemn the world, but in order that
the world might be saved through him" (John 3:16,
NRSV)

"One day as Jesus was walking along the shores of
the Sea of Galilee, he saw Simon [later called Peter] and
his brother Andrew fishing with nets, for they were com-
mercial fishermen."

"Jesus called out to them, 'Come follow me! And I
will make you fishermen for the souls of men!' They left
their nets and went along with him."

"A little farther up the beach, he saw Zebedee's sons,
James and John, in a boat mending their nets. He called
them too, and immediately they left their father in the
boat with the hired men and went with him" (Mark 1:16-
20).

If we choose to be a positive and spiritual channel through which God can do His great work, then we have chosen to be fishermen/women for the souls of men, women, and children. We will be building up treasures in heaven for ourselves.

"Do not store up for yourselves treasures on earth, where moth and rust destroy, and where thieves break in and steal. But store up for yourselves treasures in heaven, where moth and rust do not destroy, and where thieves do not break in and steal. For where your treasure is, there your heart will be also" (Matt. 6:19-21, NIV).

*   *   *   *   *

When the curtain comes down on my life, I want to believe that my life made a positive difference, that it mattered. I believe anyone who is willing to be a positive and spiritual channel through which God can do his great work will, without doubt, have lived a life that mattered. Will you join me in being a channel through which God can do his great work? Love, joy, and inner peace await you if you do.

On 14 June 1999, my oncologist told me that the Fludarabine chemotherapy had, again, put my non-Hodgkins low-grad lymphoma cancer in remission. "Thank you Lord."

*   *   *   *   *

To Christians, God has given us the Holy Bible, the standard by which we are to live our lives. "Desiderata" and the "Saint Francis of Assisi Prayer" are also great guides for living our lives, and the latter, is an excellent guideline for being a positive and spiritual channel through which God can touch the lives of those around us.

Saint Francis of Assisi Prayer

"Lord, make me an instrument
of Thy peace.
Where there is hatred,
let me sow love;
Where there is injury, pardon;
Where there is doubt, faith;
Where there is despair, hope;
Where there is darkness, light;
Where there is sadness, joy;

O Divine Master, grant that I may
not so much seek
To be consoled, as to console,
To be understood,
as to understand,
To be loved, as to love.
For it is in giving that we receive,
It is in pardoning, that
we are pardoned,
It is in dying to self
that we are born to eternal life."

—Saint Francis of Assisi

Desiderata

Go placidly amid the noise & haste, & remember what peace there may be in silence. As far as possible without surrender be on good terms with all persons. Speak your truth quietly and clearly; and listen to others, even the dull and ignorant; they too have their story. Avoid loud and aggressive persons, they are vexations to the spirit. If you compare yourself with others, you may become vain and bitter; for always there will be greater and lesser persons than yourself. Enjoy your achievements as well as your plans. Keep interested in your own career, however humble; it is a real possession in the changing fortunes of time. Exercise caution in your business affairs; for the world is full of trickery. But let this not blind you to what virtue there is; many persons strive for high ideals; and everywhere life is full of heroism. Be yourself. Especially, do not feign affection. Neither be cynical about love; for in the face of all aridity and disenchantment it is perennial as the grass. Take kindly the counsel of the years, gracefully surrendering the things of youth. Nurture strength of spirit to shield you in sudden misfortune. But do not distress yourself with imaginings. Many fears are born of fatigue and loneliness. Beyond a wholesome discipline, be gentle with yourself. You are a child of the universe, no less than the trees and stars; you have a right to be here. And whether or not it is clear to you, no doubt the universe is unfolding as it should. Therefore be at peace with God, whatever you conceive Him to be, and whatever your labors and aspirations, in the noisy confusion of life keep peace with your soul. With all its sham, drudgery and broken dreams, it is still a beautiful world. Be cheerful. Strive to be happy.

—Found in St Paul's Church in 1692

Resources

American Indian Poetry. edited by George W. Cronyn. Liveright/W. W. Norton, Co.

Carothers, Merlin R., *Power In Praise.* Escondido (Box 2518), CA. (92033-2518) Published by Merlin Carothers, 1972.

Cornell, Joseph. *Listening to Nature.* Nevada City, CA. Dawn Publications. 1987.

Ford, Judy. *Wonderful Ways to Love a Grandchild.* Berkeley, CA. Conari Press, 1997.

Frankl, Victor E., *Man's Search for Meaning.* New York, N.Y. Pocket Books. 1963.

Graham, Billy. *Angels, Gods Secret Agents.* Nashville, TN. Word Publishing. 1994.

Khan, Hazart Inayat. *Nature Meditations.* Sufi Order Publications.

Kubler-Ross, Elisabeth. *Death: The Final Stage of Growth.* Englewood Cliffs, N.J. Prentice-Hall, Inc. 1975.

McDonald, Gordon. *The Hound of Heaven—Contemporary Translation of a Timeless Masterpiece.* Lafayette, Louisiana. Vital Issues Press. 1997.

Siegel, Bernie S. Love, *Medicine & Miracles.* New York, N.Y. Harper & Row, Publishers, Inc., 1986.

The Living Bible. Wheaton, IL. Tyndale House Publishers. 1971.

The Upper Room, Daily Devotional Guide. July-August 1999, Vol. 65, No. 3, Nashville, TN.

Weil, Andrew, *Spontaneous Healing.* New York, N.Y. Alfred A. Knopf, Inc., 1995.

White Eagle. *The Path of the Soul.* Great Britain. William Clowes Limited, 1959.

White Eagle. *The Quiet Mind.* Great Britain. William Clowes Limited, 1972.

Wolfe, Linnie Marsh. *Son to the Wilderness: A Life of John Muir.* New York, N.Y. Alfred A. Knopf. 1945.

"You Are Not Alone," a tiny booklet. Unity Village, Missouri. Unity School Of Christianity.

We welcome comments from our readers.
Feel free to write to us at the following address:

Editorial Department
Huntington House Publishers
P.O. Box 53788
Lafayette, LA 70505

or visit our website at:

www.huntingtonhousebooks.com

More Good Books

from

Huntington House Publishers

The Myth of ADHD and
Other Learning Disabilities
Parenting Without Ritalin
by Dr. Jan Strydom and Susan du Plessis
If your child has been diagnosed with ADHD or some other behavior disorder, be careful. This diagnosis could be false. The authors of this book explain how parents can teach their children the skills of concentration and self-control without drugging them into submission. With over 25 years in education, consultation and research of learning and behavior problems, Dr. Strydom has helped many parents find ways to help their children.

ISBN 1-56384-180-0

Cloning of the American Mind
Eradicating Morality Through Education
by B. K. Eakman
Why are our children having problems learning? Find out what is really happening in our public schools. *Are the various educational programs being touted really helping our children learn? What is electronic profiling? How does psychologically based teaching hurt our children? Is the teacher really qualified to determine that my child needs Ritalin — isn't that a diagnosis for a doctor to decide? Are teachers really being taught to teach the basics that every child should know?* These are just a few questions every parent should be asking our school officials. The research and thorough documentation by the author will open the door to what is really happening to our educational system. What can we as parents do to ensure our children are taught the basics? Check out Chapter 4 — you'll find many tips and suggestions for parents to work with the school establishment (school boards, education committees, legislative, etc.) to combat the programs that don't work. *Cloning of the American Mind* has been described by one radio host as *one of the most comprehensive books on education.* Thomas Sowell, *New York Post* (September 4, 1998 issue) writes that *"Parents who do not realize what a propaganda apparatus the public schools have become should read* Cloning of the American Mind *by B.K. Eakman"*

ISBN 1-56384-147-9

The Cookbook:
Health Begins in Him
by Terry Dorian, Ph.D.

The is an action plan for optimal health and hormone balance! *The Cookbook: Health Begins in Him* offers a dietary regime and food preparation based on both scientific studies and biblical guidelines. Under Dr. Dorian's directions, whole-foods chef Rita M. Thomas has created one hundred and seventy recipes with instructions on:

• How to prepare breads, pastas, cereals, and waffles with freshly milled flour.

• How to prepare desserts that help maintain optimal health.

• How to prepare raw vegetable dishes, raw vegetable dressings, cooked vegetables, grain-based casseroles, beans and grains, fermented dishes, and soy foods.

ISBN 1-56384-127-4

Wired to Work
Answering the Two Most Important Questions in Life
by Vince D'Acchioli

Have you ever wondered what God's plan for your life is? Would you be more successful and happy if you were fulfilling your destiny? Vince D'Acchioli helps you discover *how* and *why* God made you and shows that your were **born** to succeed! Stephen Strang, CEO and Founder of Strang Communications Co., says *"So open the toolbox ... and get started. You won't find a more useful resource.* John C. Maxwell, Founder of the Injoy Group, says that *"Vince D'Acchioli has a unique and powerfully effective way of leading men and women to a discovery of God's plan for their life. Don't miss out on the importance of this life changing message."* Vince D'Acchioli is the Founder of On Target Ministries, based in Monument, Colorado, who has over the past few years, conducted seminars, workshops, church services, and Promise Keepers rallies that have impacted people's lives across the U.S. and Canada.

ISBN 1-56384-191-6

From the Darkness
One Woman's to Nobility
by Connie Morris

From the Darkness is a *"...compelling story of what faith in Jesus Christ can do to change a person's life for the better. Connie Morris's life is a testament to the power of that faith,"* says U.S. Congressman Jerry Morgan. From a life of sexual abuse and violence at the age of 12 to a miraculous conversion and recovery, Connie Morris's remarkable story will inspire and transform you.

ISBN 1-56384-194-0

Pursuing the Permanent
Meeting the Part of You That Lives Forever
by Jayne Reizner

Amidst hectic schedules and fast-track careers, people in modern society spend most of their time focusing on responsibilities at work and home, leaving little energy for spiritual reflection and meditation. In *Pursuing the Permanent,* author Jane Reizner stresses the importance of nourishing the innermost part of ourselves — our souls. She addresses pertinent spiritual questions about life, including: *How can I live with an eternal perspective? How can I pursue ordinary, everyday routines with passion? How can I live in harmony with God and others? Pursuing the Permanent* entreats us to ignore society's definition of happiness and instead focus on the needs of our souls. Then, we can learn the secret of living life on earth with an eternal perspective that emanates from the core of our being.

ISBN 1-56384-126-6

Another Look
by R.L. Brandt

Reverend Brandt asks us to ponder and re-examine our most cherished interpretations of Scripture. Every chapter is replete with profoundly penetrating insight — taking *another look* at Faith, Satan, God, Truth, Repentance, Grace, Heaven. As each of us interprets Scripture in the light of our own mind-set, we often see in Scripture what is not there or we miss what is really there. It is therefore imperative that all of us take another look and let the Holy Spirit guide us to the true interpretation.

ISBN 1-56384-183-5

The Desert Rat
The Remarkable Story of Aileen Coleman
by Annette Adams

Aileen Coleman has been celebrated by the princely and noble as well as the lowly and oppressed. She is known by many names — "The Angel of the Desert," "Blood Brother to the Bedouin," or A`raisa," the leader. One dignitary lovingly referred to her as "one of the greatest servants God ever put on His earth." Aileen Coleman humbly shuns such "pretentious and flowery titles" and answers only the much more prosaic name — "The Desert Rat." The story of Aileen Coleman, her faithfulness and servanthood through four decades as a medical missionary in the Middle East could change your life forever.

ISBN 1-56384-193-2

Evangelism That Works
by Phil Derstine

Phil Derstine brings a fresh, innovative approach to soul winning, blending biblical truths with eye-opening personal experience. With a plan that is simple but profoundly effective, he teaches you how to share your faith with others. It is his love for people and distinctive burden for souls that have taken him to the streets with the message of hope.

ISBN 1-56384-191-9

101 Biblical Secrets for Success
Financial, Emotional, and Spiritual
by Sherwood Jansen, Esq.

101 Biblical Secrets for Success is comprised of 101 easy-to-read chapters. The author demonstrates that the age-old philosophies from the Old and New Testaments are ever current and applicable to everyday situations. Subjects include: *Secrets to Attaining Happiness, Ways to Health, Keys to Effective Communication, How to Put Passion into Your Work, Cures for Insomnia, The Importance of Money, Prosperity for Your Family, Defeating Discouragement, The Wisdom Found in Women, Time Management, Thinking Thoughts of Greatness.*

ISBN 1-56384-176-2

What Would They Say?
The Founding Fathers on Current Issues
by Glen Gorton

Thomas Jefferson, John Hancock, George Washington — If these men could once again walk through the halls of Congress, surveying the present scene, what would they say? We were told by the Clinton administration that things like honor and integrity don't matter as long as the rate of inflation is kept down. Our Founding Fathers disagree. They believed that high moral character is an essential ingredient of leadership. Into the heated atmosphere of today's social and political crossfire comes a refreshingly new point of view from — the Founding Fathers. This is not another analysis of the men and their times, but rather, the penetrating and concise testimony of America's greatest heroes. Herein lies the strength of this 240 page anthology: the Founding Fathers themselves. *What Would They Say?* is divided into three parts: (1) Part One has quotes under topics covering Character, Patriotism, Federal Power, Crime, Taxes, Education, Gun Control, Welfare, Term Limits, and Religion; (2) Part Two gives the reader an animated and personal glimpse into the life of each of the 28 men quoted; and (3) Part Three contains a copy of the *Declaration of Independence,* the *US Constitution,* and the *Bill of Rights.*

ISBN 1-56384-146-0

The Separation of Church and State
Has America Lost Its Moral Compass?
By Stephen Strehle

Can Religion be divorced from politics? Author Stephen Strehle contends that the path of righteousness and moral accountability is the roadway to our nation's prosperity. Our inalienable rights grew out of the western religious tradition of natural law, egalitarianism out of the universal scope of the Christian Gospel, democracy out of the polity of Puritan congregations;, capitalism out of the Protestant work ethic. Human beings cannot live in self-sufficient autonomy. God is over all, in all, and through all.

ISBN 1-56384-180-0

The Coming Collision
Global Law vs. U.S. Liberties
by James L. Hirsen, Ph.D.

Are Americans' rights being abolished by International Bureaucrats? Global activists have wholeheartedly embraced environmental extremism, international governance, radical feminism, and New Age mysticism with the intention of spreading their philosophies worldwide by using the powerful weight of international law. Noted international and constitutional attorney James L. Hirsen says that a small group of international bureaucrats are devising and implementing a system of world governance that is beginning to adversely and irrevocably affect the lives of everyday Americans.

Paperback   ISBN 1-56384-157-6
Hardcover   ISBN 1-56384-163-0

Government by Decree
From President to Dictator
Through Executive Orders
by James L. Hirsen, Ph.D.

Could Americans lose their constitutional rights and be forced to live under martial law with the stroke of open? Sound like fiction? Wrong! Right now, through the use of a tool called an executive order, the President of the United States has the power to institute broad, invasive measures that could directly impact the lives of average, everyday Americans. What might trigger the exercise of this type of awesome power? Any number of things could, but for certain, a crisis, real or manufactured, is the most frightening prospect.

ISBN 1-56384-166-5

Government by Political Spin
by David J. Turell, M.D.

Political Spin has been raised to a fine art in this country. These highly paid "spin doctors" use sound bites and ambiguous rhetoric to, at best, influence opinions, and at worst, completely mislead the public. *Government by Political Spin* clearly describes the giant PR program used by Washington officials to control the information to American citizens and maintain themselves in power.

ISBN 1-56384-172-X

The Hidden Dangers of the Rainbow
by Constance Cumbey

This nationwide best-seller paved the way for all other books on the subject of the New Age movement. Constance Cumbey's book reflects years of in-depth and extensive research. She clearly demonstrates the movement's supreme purpose: to subvert our Judeo-Christian foundation and create a one-world order through a complex network of occult organizations. Cumbey details how these various organizations are linked together by common mystical experiences. The author discloses who and where the leaders of this movement are and discusses their secret agenda to destroy our way of life.

ISBN 0-910311-03-X

The Deadly Deception
Freemasonry Exposed..
By One of Its Top Leaders
by Jim Shaw and Tom McKenny

This is the story of one man's climb to the top, the top of the "Masonic mountain." A climb that uncovered many "secrets" enveloping the popular fraternal order of Freemasonry. Shaw brings to life the truth about Freemasonry, both good and bad, and for the first time ever, reveals the secretive Thirty-Third Degree initiation.

ISBN 0-910311-54-4

Inside the New Age Nightmare
by Randall Baer

Are your children safe from the New Age movement? This former New Age leader, one of the world's foremost experts in crystals, brings to light the darkest of the darkness that surrounds the New Age movement. The week that Randall Baer's original book was released, he met with a puzzling and untimely death—his car ran off a mountain pass. His death is still regarded as suspicious.

ISBN 0-910311-58-7

Salt Series   ISBN 1-56384-022-7

Spiritual Warfare
The Invisible Invasion
by Thomas R. Horn

Thomas Horn illustrates through fresh and powerful new insights that while demonic activity has frequently been overlooked, the close collaboration between social architects and ancient evil powers has at times allowed demons to control the machine of world governments, and the moral and social trends of a nation.

ISBN 1-56384-129-0

En Route to Global Occupation
A High Ranking Government Liaison Exposes the Secret Agenda for World Unification
by Gary H. Kah

Kah warns that national sovereignty will soon be a thing of the past. Political forces around the world are now cooperating in unprecedented fashion to achieve their goal of uniting the people of this planet under a New World Order. High-ranking government liaison Gary Kah was dismissed from his position when he refused to "keep silent" and warns that national sovereignty will soon be a thing of the past. Invited to join WCPA (World Constitution and Parliamentary Association), the author was involved in the planning and implementation of a one-world government. For the skeptical observer, the material in this should serve as ample evidence that the drive to create a one-world government is for real. Reproductions of the original documentation are included.

ISBN 0-910311-97-8

New World Order
The Ancient Plan of Secret Societies
by William T. Still

For thousands of years, secret societies have cultivated an ancient plan which has powerfully influenced world events. Until now, this secret plan has remained hidden from view. This book presents new evidence that a military take-over of the U.S. was considered by some in the administration of one of our recent presidents. Although averted, the forces behind it remain in secretive positions of power.

ISBN 0-910311-64-1

ABCs of Globalism
A Vigilant Christians Glossary
by Debra Rae

Do you know what organizations are working together to form a new world order? Unlike any book on today's market, the *ABCs of Globalism* is a single volume reference that belongs in every concerned Christian's home. It allows easy access to over one hundred entries spanning a number of fields–religious, economic, educational, environmental, and more. Each item features an up-to-date overview, coupled with a Biblical perspective.

ISBN 1-56384-140-1

Liberalism
Fatal Consequences
by W. A. Borst, Ph.D.

Liberalism indicted! *Liberalism: Fatal Consequences* will arm conservatives of all kinds (Christians, Orthodox Jews, patriots, concerned citizens) with the necessary historical and intellectual ammunition to fight the culture war on any front as it exposes the hypocrisy of liberalism.

"...an excellent critical examination of the issues that threaten to divide our nation." —President Roche, Hillsdale College

ISBN 1-56384-153-3

That Kind Can Never Change ... Can They?
One Man' s Struggle with His Homosexuality
by Victor J. Adamson

Author Victor Adamson shares this true story of his struggle to understand and then overcome his homosexuality. Was he born this way or was he conditioned by abuse, environment, and circumstances? Could God love him in spite of the lifestyle he was leading? *Was it possible for someone like him to change?* This true story of his path to victory is shared so that others may know that nothing is impossible with God.

ISBN 1-56384-175-4

Gender Agenda:
Redefining Equality
by Dale O'Leary

All women have the right to choose motherhood as their primary vocation. The radical feminists' movement poses a threat to this right — In the early 1970s, a small group of radical feminists weren't satisfied with equal rights — they wanted to restructure society as a whole. When mainstream women refused to accept the feminist world view, these radical feminists turned to the legislative process to enforce their agenda. And, under the guise of conventions for the rights of women, the United Nations is now actively promoting a radical feminist ideology. In *The Gender Agenda: Redefining Equality,* author Dale O'Leary takes a spirited look at the feminist movement, its influence on legislation, and its subsequent threat to the ideals of family, marriage and motherhood. By shedding light on the destructiveness of the feminist world view, *The Gender Agenda* exposes the true agenda of the feminist movement.

ISBN 1-56384-122-3

My Genes Made Me Do It
A Scientific Look at Sexual Orientation
by Neil and Briar Whitehead

Is homosexuality biologically fated? If it is, shouldn't gays be allowed to marry? Can gays change their sexual orientation and become heterosexual? What does science really say about homosexuality and sexual orientation? Taking a mainstream scientific position, this clear, comprehensive and accessible book concludes that a close and careful examination of the scientific evidence does not support the current views that homosexuality is genetic, intrinsic, or fixed. Neil and Briar Whitehead have been researching homosexuality for over eight years. Neil is a research scientist with a Ph.D. in biochemistry. Briar is a writer. They have found many people who feel that gays are "born that way" — but few who understand enough about genetics and human biology to mount a thorough defense of the facts.

ISBN 1-56384-165-7

Married
Happily Ever After?
by Dudley Bienvenu, Jr.

Is staying in love for a lifetime and living happily ever after mere fantasy, or is it really possible? There is an epidemic sweeping our country, destroying our marriages and families. It's called divorce. With over fifty percent of all marriages and sixty percent of second marriages now ending in divorce, millions of lives are being affected. *What's missing? What's the answer?* Author Dudley Bienvenu says, *"You can learn how to 'love the one you're with' always and forever."* For almost two decades, Bienvenu has utilized his teaching and counseling gifts in helping to strengthen and restore marriages. Many of the techniques and lessons he uses to help couples are revealed in this book.

ISBN 1-56384-189-4

The Highest Calling ... Fatherhood
by Michael D. Barnes

This unique book explores the biblical approach to the high calling of fatherhood. It is a handy, step-by-step instruction book for fathers who want to teach their children the ways of God. Dr. Joseph Umidi, Professor of Ministry of Regent Divinity School says, *"I am recommending this book to all my pastoral students, my parishioners, and those wanting to know how to 'turn the hearts of the fathers to the children.' This book is full of hope and will breathe life into your situation."*

ISBN 1-56384-186-X

Are We Living In the End Time?
Prophetic Events Destined to Impact Your World
by Rod Hall

Biblical Prophecy and its revelance to our World. What are the prophectic events destined to impact our world? Wars! Famine! Earthquakes! Massive destruction around the globe! From his 30 years of intense research and study of the prophecies of the Bible, the author shows us the many societal trends and world events taking shape today. The Word of God is the foundation of all knowledge, understanding, and hope. It is a guide to living and provides a worldview that will become our future reality.

ISBN 0-933451-48-2

Fiction

The 3 Loves of Charlie Delaney
by Joey W. Kiser

A delightful story of first love, innocence, heartbreak, and redemption. Kiser uses his pen to charm and enchant but most of all...to remind.

ISBN 0-933451-45-8

A Fruitful Field
by Cliff Schrage, Jr

First-time novelist, Cliff Schrage, takes us from the abyss of heartbreak to the fervor of redemption. A modern novel that brings us a fresh awareness of God's compassion.

ISBN 1-56384-182-7

Patriots
Surviving the Coming Collapse
by James Wesley, Rawles

Patriots, a fast-paced novel by James Wesley, Rawles is more than a novel — it's a survival manual. Could you survive a total collapse of civilization — a modern Dark Ages? Would you be prepared for the economic collapse, the looting, riots, panic, and complete breakdown of our infrastructure?

"More than just a novel, this book is filled with tips on how to survive what we all hope isn't coming to America."

—Jefferson Adams, *The Idaho Observer*
ISBN 1-56384-155-X

The Prophecy—2024
by Kirt R. Poovey

The Prophecy — a novel set in the near future using contemporary issues by taking real-life events of today and interweaving them into an interesting and believable story with an underlying Christian theme. Written to awaken and educate readers to the ongoing atrocities occurring in society, and to encourage them to amke a difference for change. It's about romance ... it's about fear ... it's about a fight for freedom ... about intrigue, tragedy, power, but most of all — it's about hope and life and placing our trust in God. *The Prophecy* embraces a strong, conservative, moral viewpoint and shows the tragedies of a tyrannical government.

ISBN 1-56384-197-5